Tomas D. Andres

UNDERSTANDING
FILIPINO VALUES
A Management Approach

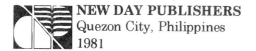

NEW DAY PUBLISHERS
Quezon City, Philippines
1981

Understanding Filipino Values acquaints the reader with the Filipino value systems and Philippine business management problems, trends, and issues as they affect and relate to productivity and organizational effectiveness. Emphasis is placed on the process of value clarification and redirection to equip the reader with the skill in choosing those values with which to make decisions and strategies to effect productivity and organizational effectiveness. Filipino value concepts, principles, techniques, systems, and approaches are applied to the problems most commonly met in business management and organizational development.

This book encourages the reader to become more sensitive to and concerned with Filipino values, enabling him to restructure and reorient these values intelligently for business management effectivity and productivity. The reader's ability to think critically on current and emerging issues and problems affecting productivity and organizational effectiveness on the basis of a fully understood Filipino value system is further developed.

This book is intended for individual reading as well as to serve as text in Administrative Processes and Organizational Behavior, Human Behavior in Organization, Organizational Development, Humanities, Philosophy, Business Ethics, and Character Education courses.

Tomas Quintin D. Andres

Ateneo de Manila University
February 11, 1981

ACKNOWLEDGMENTS

The writer wishes to acknowledge the authorities and practitioners in the fields of philosophy, anthropology, sociology, psychology and business management, and other related disciplines who shared their insights; as well as those others who helped shape and complete this work. In the preparation of this work, therefore, the writer wishes to give due recognition to the following:

Reverend Father Francis Senden, C.I.C.M., former director of Asian Social Institute and my former professor at the San Carlos Seminary; Dr. Romeo Carleta, my former professor at the Far Eastern University Institute of Graduate Studies; Reverend Fr. Francisco de Pamplona, O.F.M.Cap., former professor of Asian Social Institute and my colleague in the Capuchin Order; Professor Antonio Carion, chairman of the Marketing Department of De La Salle University; Reverend Father Robert Bomeisl, S.J. and Fr. Thomas Fitzpatrick, S.J. of the Ateneo Graduate School of Business; Mrs. Gloria F. Rodriguez and Miss Bezalie P. Bautista of New Day Publishers; my former students in the graduate schools of De La Salle University and Ateneo de Manila University;

My wife, Pilar Corazon and kids, Thomas Philamer, Pilar Philamer, Pierreangelo Philamer, and Lord Philamer.

CONTENTS

To my **FATHER**
whose values as a Filipino
led him to give his life
for his family, God, and country

The Filipino Philosophy of Values

During the past years, many sociologists, anthropologists, and psychologists have written books and articles about Filipino values. These works call for a development of a Filipino philosophy of values so that its ultimate causes and principles be manifested.

Today, the need for a solid Filipino philosophy of values is urgent in order to serve as a fundamental basis not only to speculation of the different sciences but also to the practice of our Filipino patriotism, management, and identity.

The first question we have to tackle, however, is, Does a Filipino philosophy of values exist? By philosophy, one may mean the following:

(1) any doctrine that proposes a wisdom destined to conduct men toward their end by making known the origin and destination of all things, whether that wisdom is acquired naturally or revealed by God;

(2) an ensemble of truths that can be discovered by the human mind left to its own devices, without however excluding the influence of non-rational data;

(3) a body of doctrine that possesses the coherence and certitude proper to the sciences as understood in the modern sense. Philosophy in such an understanding proceeds from a simple and absolutely certain point of departure to draw out the entire sequence of its propositions in a necessary order.

If we consider the notion that a Filipino philosophy of values exists and take the meaning of philosophy in the first sense, we

1

find no difficulty in accepting it since it signifies simply that the Filipino mind has some set of teachings and principles which guide him to salvation. If we understand it in the second sense, a problem poses itself only theoretically. The solution to this difficulty consists in offering that religion or revelation an influence over the Filipino philosophy of values.

The Filipino Philosophy of Values: A Hybrid

The Filipino people have a reputation for being cultural hybrids. This is most evident in our art, cities, behavior, fashions among women, business and government practices.

The Filipino philosophy of values must be founded on life and experience. To be scientific, it must be constructed "from below," not derived "from above." The ideal goal of a philosophy of values as a science is an objectively justified set of principles which is fundamental enough to hold for all particular situations.

Culturally, the population of the Philippines reflects the great variety of external influences which have impinged upon and blended with the original Malay culture: Arabian, Chinese, Indo-Chinese, Hindu-Indonesian, Spanish-Catholic, and American-Protestant. However, the cultural matrix of the modern Filipino was already there at the time of the Spanish *conquista* in the middle of the 16th century and may well have been there a thousand years before that. Cultural traits have been borrowed somehow, but combined in such a way that the result is distinctly "Filipino." The basic temperament, the lifestyle, the outlook that make up the culture of the Filipino today were already there four centuries ago.[1] Thus, we cannot underevaluate the strength of the traditional features of Filipino behavior and belief. The lineal village, the strong family unit, the kinship relationships extended through marriage and leadership, the authority vested on family heads and elders were all existent even before the Western contact.

Historically, the Philippines has drunk from the fount of three physical and cultural words—the Asian, the Pacific, and the Occidental. The Filipino traditional culture moreover is a synthesis of three mainstreams—the Malay which in itself is a hybrid, the Chinese Mind, and the Indian Art. The structure of communal life, native and imported ceramic art, behavioral patterns, beliefs, and values are evidences of this.

2

What is a Filipino?

Ask any Filipino to define a Filipino, and he will be perplexed, confused, stupefied, and puzzled. He will probably answer, "The Filipino is a citizen of the Philippines." Or "the Filipino is a Negrito." Is the Filipino the irredeemable, indolent, incapable *indio* presented by some Spanish propagandists during the colonial times? Is the Filipino the little brown "American" who imitates and assimilates whatever is foreign and blue zeal? Is the Filipino the premature Negrito in Zambales or the Igorot in the rice terraces of the Mountain Province? Is the Filipino the peace-loving Tasaday discovered by Elizalde in Mindanao? In my other book, I wrote:[2]

The Filipino is all these and more! The Filipino is the imponderable unity and uniqueness of diverse races, richness, and idiosyncracies. The Filipino is the legacy of the multi-racial humanity. The Filipino is the monument of the Malays, the Spaniards, the Americans, the Japanese, the Chinese, the Hindus, the Dutch, and the Englishman all united into one. The Filipino is the Christian formed by Spain who has a centralized government, the Roman Law, and Latin alphabet. The Filipino is the Chinese who knows the art of mining, metallurgy gun-powder making, porcelain, and pottery production. The Filipino is the American who drinks beer, plays basketball, has democratic temperament and public school system, speaks English, and sees Hollywood films. Yet prior to all this, the Filipino is the Malay who had a village government ruled by oral and written laws promulgated by the datu, recognized a supreme being and lesser deities in his animo-deist religion, used juices, herbs and oils for medical purposes, and was expert in carvings and handicrafts industries. Today, the Filipino is the *Filipino* who is himself, a Malay-Indonesia negrito distilled with European and American cultures and races; an individual well-gifted in friendship, understanding, letters, arts and sciences, sports and pursuit of excellence; a Christian gentleman; an avid lover of democracy; and a personality gradually discovering his identity.

The Filipino is all these and *more!* More, because he can develop the talents and innate qualities and he can surpass the legacies of his ancestors and predecessors. But he can never renounce the European and American cultural and racial legacies in him. They are in his flesh and blood. They are a part of his being. To renounce them means to renounce a part of his own identity and personality. The Filipino is Asian but he is also European. The Filipino is Oriental but he is also Occidental. He cannot be entirely eastern; he is also western.

If we are to dissect the Filipino, it will turn out like this:

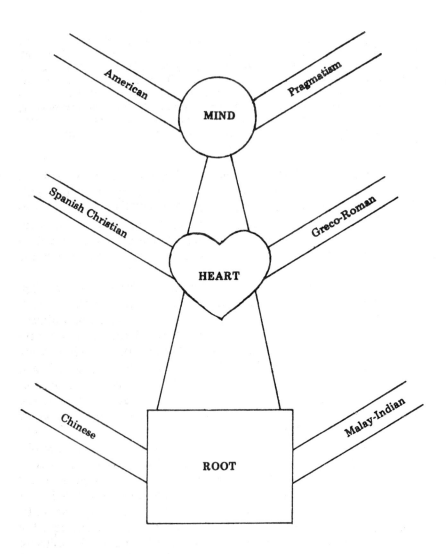

The Roots of the Filipino

The Malay

The roots of the Filipino are Malay and Chinese. The Malay temper is the main component of Filipino culture. To understand the Malay is to understand the Filipino. He is himself a hybrid of the Indian, Persian, Arab, Thai, and mainly, the Chinese of the Chou period. Carmen Guerrero-Nakpil writes:[3]

The premier Malay characteristic is a certain likeableness that most Westerners describe as charm, which is in turn really a compound of the old-fashioned virtues, like faith, hope and charity. The Malay is as trusting as a child, naturally tolerant, forbearing and kind. He laughs a good deal, not the least frequently at himself, and is convinced that tomorrow, if the fates will it, everything will be better. His frequent insolvency is due to an overweening generosity, and if he is usually unwilling to press a point, it is out of a certain largeness of heart. He is brave almost to the point of recklessness and, of course, he is nothing if not eloquent.

Readiness to adjust to a new situation and desire to be above all nice are the two strongest strains in the Malay character. This pliability had been demonstrated, all through the thousand years of the Malay recorded history: long migrations, painful colonizations, warm weather, and starchy diet. He has always been willing to accept any new concept or a new master and reconcile it to his old customs and live with it happily.

The Malay has borrowed the divinity of kings from the Assyrian-Babylonian and secularism and humanism from the modern west. His religion is a mixture of Hinduism, Islam, and Christianity.

The Malay respect for "niceness" is remarkable in his endeavor to avoid not so much sin or crime as impropriety. Though his Catholicism or devotion to the Koran inspires him to be virtuous, what matters to him is to be nice, agreeable, and pleasant. For him, frankness is a breach of courtesy; punctuality, a sign of coarseness. He is a natural conformist, with the typical Malay personality of mercurial improvisation.

The Malay is the world's baby of nature because nature has always been bountiful to him. His love for fiesta is exorbitant. What matters is "the lovely here-and-now." A five-year socioeconomic program or a two-year infrastructure program is too arduous a task for him. It is the carrot, not the stick, that motivates him best. Unemployment is not really a social problem for him because most of the unemployment is by choice. In spite all these, the Malay was once an empire builder (the Madjapahit and the Sri-Vishaya) and he may, under the right stars, become at least a confederacy again.

The Malay is frivolous. His religious rituals and ceremonies become an occasion for merry-making and enjoyment. His summit meetings and conferences are liable to dissolve into a litany of green jokes and bawdy stories about dancing girls. His highest praise is that a man is *marunong makisama* (easy to get along with).

These traits of the Malay are probably brought on by environmental condition. The Filipino is still of the stubborn Malay blood, despite the recombined evaporated "improvement." The Malay Filipino has been conditioned to expect defeat. His history consists of a series of defeats.

The Filipino has been conditioned to think *small*. *Nacionalismo* (patriotism) and *orgullo nacional* (national pride) were not made part of his vocabulary. Thus, the steadiest thing in his fluid world is his family ties—its rituals and fetishes. The family is his best social security system. He was taught to sing sad songs about his pathetic plight—"I was poorly born on top of the mountain"; "my nipa hut is very small"; "negritos of the mountain, what kind of food do you eat?"

The Chinese

The second component of the Filipino root is Chinese. Chinese traders started coming to the Philippines in the latter part of the T'ang dynasty (618-907 A.D.). Before its close, between 2000 to 3000 Chinese had established residence here. Pottery making and agricultural development came to the Philippines through the Chinese. Thus, most of the Filipino farm and household implements are Chinese; the methods used in agriculture, marketing, and the domestic milieu are Chinese.

According to Carmen Guerrero-Nakpil,[4] about 10% of Filipino genes is Chinese. The Chinese mind, a blend of philosophy and pragmatism, has been transplanted into the Filipino psyche. Patience and perseverance, hardiness and foresight, frugality and thrift have been infused into the Filipino character by the indomitable Chinese traders and craftsmen who came and stayed; and were absorbed into the mainstream of Filipino life. The Confucian philosophy accounts for most of the values they inculcated. The Chinese ideal of *filial piety*, the emphasis on man as a *social being* and *"sageliness within and kingliness without"* ideal have been carried over into Filipino life. Thus for a Filipino, relationship between parents and children, and lateral relatives is a matter of *ethics* and *honor*. Getting along with one's neighbors is a fundamental prerequisite to prosperity, happiness, and human existence. *Sageliness* or self-improvement by cultivation of virtue, personal worth, and wisdom is evident in our national passion for education. Elaborate dress, ritual and etiquette, propriety and wealth, and class distinctions are witnesses to *kingliness*.

The Indian

The Indian elements in the Filipino lie mainly in art, manners, beliefs, and language. Through the Sri-Vishaya Empire of Sumatra and the Madjapahit Empire of Djawa, Indian cultural influences which affected the cultural development of the Filipinos flowed into the Philippines. The ancient Filipino religious beliefs are features of the Brahman religion of India. Folk beliefs such as one's friends or relatives will die if the person dreams his teeth have fallen out, are Indian. In some way, the Filipinos are really "indios."

The Heart of the Filipino

The heart of the Filipino is Spanish Christian. Christianization and social organization along Western lines leading to political unity and to the Western institution called nation were contributions of the Spaniards to the Filipinos. The religion of 80% of Filipinos is Spanish Catholicism—a religion based on folk christianity mixed with pre-Spanish superstitions and pagan beliefs. In fact, the language of the Philippine Revolution and of its leaders who were Europeanized *ilustrados* was Spanish.

Other contributions were the Spanish law and Greco Roman culture. Many of the value judgments, or the social standards of Filipino life are Spanish in origin. The quixoticism of Filipinos—a combination of generosity and arrogance—is Spanish. *Delicadeza* is a concept that is typically Spanish. Gentility or the emphasis on appearance, reputation, privilege, and status are all Spanish. Thus, the elegance and gentility of the Filipinas who win beauty contests abroad.

The Mind of the Filipino

The mind of the Filipino is American. American influence in the Philippines actually started in 1792. It can be traced back to what is called in American history, the China Trade. Some of the American elements are the public health system, road system, mass education, English language, modern mechanics and techniques of Westernized democracy, public service and administration, presidential system, congress, and municipal government.

The American regime literally shocked the Filipino. What with so many centuries inside a monastic culture, when suddenly the Filipino was exposed to Hollywood life! The Filipino became *pragmatic.* When before he had a docile and obedient mind, now he learned to ask two questions: "Does it work?" "What has he done?" The Filipino was influenced to develop a system of thought wherein what matters is concern *with things, with quantities* and *with achievements;* and not the Oriental's "What do the others feel?" or "What is the thinking of others?" Nor the Spanish "Who is he?", "What can it do?" became the most important question.

Another American ingredient in the Filipino is the Protestant ethics of rationality, of questioning, of independent thinking, and of direct communication.

The Filipino Value Orientation

The Filipino has frequently been diagnosed as one suffering from value crisis. That is, he is ambivalent in his convictions and distrustful of his competence. He is Asian by birth and geographical setting but matured within a western matrix.

The Filipino value orientation today is more outer-directed than inner-directed. We prefer foreign models to structure our thinking, our management style, our decision-making and problem-solving process; to establish our confidence; and to justify our competence. That is why foreign-packaged management systems and training programs are marketed in the Philippines. Why do we have to demonstrate our potentialities in terms of foreign competence? Why do we seek validation of our achievement and abilities by the Western criteria?

This outer-directedness of our value orientation indicates an inner *inferiority complex.* This sense of inferiority wrought in the Filipino mind by the Spaniards is the four-hundred-year-old suspicion developing into certainty that because one is native and brown and small-nosed and Asian, he is not as good as the white man. Kozuki Koyama described the Filipino as a person with four histories and four cultures.[5] Malay, Spanish, American, and Japanese cultures permeate the Filipino personality. He is a creation of centuries of diverse social, economic, cultural, political, and psychological stresses. He is reputed to be lazy and diffident, yet, he has quite consistently been willing, ready and able to compete given half a chance.[6]

He is known to be a spendthrift, if he comes from the Tagalog region, the Visayas or Pampanga; but an incorrigible tightwad if he comes from the northern provinces. He can be illiterate, if he comes from a miserable rural family; but he can also be a savant like Rizal, Recto, Marcos if he comes from a middle class family close to the arteries of education. He can be an impoverished father cooped up with his family in a tiny nipa hut in the barrio, or a wealthy and powerful aristocrat living in a magnificent mansion at Forbes Park.

Today, the Filipino is at the crossroad of trying to define his identity. After the Spanish and American tango, he is trying to integrate his indigenous culture with his Spanish and American cultural inheritance.

Typology of Filipino Value Orientation

A. *Ultimate ends:* individual self, individual family kinship, prosperity and happiness in its holistic sense, family and individual prestige and fame.

B. *Character Structure and Life Organization:*
1. The financially successful man-image who has achievements without much hardship; who is Christlike but also mundane enough to enjoy the fruits of his work.
2. Virtues: shrewd, acquisitive, calculating, modestly ambitious but not too hardworking, manipulative of persons and things, cooperative.

C. *Person:* inherent worth and dignity of person; a son of God with an immortal soul and infinite value.

D. *Competition:* competition is inevitable in life but must be avoided if possible; if it cannot be avoided, one must come out a winner by hook or by crook; if working with competitors is advantageously good, work with them.

E. *Cooperation:* stress on mutual aid, service with ulterior motives.

F. *Wealth and property:* frugality and extravagance; my property is mine, your property is ours; public property is mine; a symbol of respectability, prestige; some things are valuated quantitatively in monetary units; a comfortable level of living regarded as desirable.

G. *Social change, intellectual inquiry, and creativity:* resistance to social change; not so inquisitive about technology; ultra-conservative in substantial matters but ultra-progressive in accidental things; psychological blocks to creativity.

✿

REFERENCE NOTES

[1]Carmen Guerrero-Nakpil, "Filipino Cultural and Foreign Influences." (Lecture delivered during the 15th International Conference on Social Welfare, on its seminar in Socio-Economic Perspective on Philippines, Davao City, September 2 & 5, 1978.)

[2]Tomas Quintin D. Andres, *New Dimensions in Philippine Christianity* (Pasay City: Daughters of St. Paul, 1973), pp. 177-178.

[3]Nakpil, pp. 2-3.

[4]Ibid., pp. 4-7.

[5]Kozuki Koyama, *Waterbuffalo Theology* (New York: Doubleday and Co., 1975), p. 8.

[6]Horacio de la Costa, "Reflections on Philippine Economic Development," *The Journal* (1976), p. 18.

Filipino Value Systems Analysis

Socio-cultural values are those considered conducive or essential to the welfare of a group. They constitute models or goals of personal behavior in social interaction. They are common to the members of a given social group and are the people's concept of what is desirable; the basis of choice among alternatives; direct interest, attention, or emphasis. They are what people see, hear, perceive, and appreciate.

Values have the following qualities: 1) they have a conceptual element; 2) they are affectively charged, with actual or potential emotional mobilization; 3) they are criteria by which goals are chosen; and 4) they are important.

The four-fold test of values in a culture are: extensiveness, duration, intensity, and the prestige of value-carriers.

Value-System is a configuration of culture, the dominant motivations and basic principles of people's behavior; the cultural ethics that binds the people together, their views and propositions about the nature of things, about the rightness or wrongness, desirability or undesirability, appropriateness or inappropriateness of actions; their concept of what is important; the desired reactions and responses to situations; their attitudes towards themselves and others, towards nature, the universe, and God; their perception of reality, their explanation of events; the meaning they attach to things.

11

What is Value Systems Analysis?

Value Systems Analysis is an innovative approach to both understanding and coping with the differences that exist between and among people, groups and even cultures. This approach affirms and recognizes the legitimacy of differences in people and prescribes synergistic therapy and treatment for each system.

Value systems reflect natural differences. Every individual responds to a value system with which he can identify and which will reveal his "coping system." People are different and respond to different kinds of systems.

Value systems deal with how we decide, what we value as a coping system; it is not *what* we value, such as car or jewelry. Two persons can value the *same thing* but for different reasons; thus it would be the *same value content*, but *different coping systems*. A value system, therefore, is a method that man uses to solve his problems, cope with his environment. This involves looking into not only how individuals differ, but how cultures differ; how man as a psychological being has evolved. From birth, man moves into different coping systems.

Value Systems Analysis deals with all the procedures within the organization loop—recruitment, selection, placement, training, internal management, and external marketing. Cultural and geographical differences show up in Value Systems Analysis. Understanding a person's value system enables us to communicate more effectively. It helps a recruitment officer match a job with a person whose value system is the same, rather than expecting the worker to change his value system.

A perceptive manager will learn to differentiate among the different values and behavior of people. Managers who are unaware of their employees' different value systems commit the mistake in designing a system of management that is good for *them*, not one that is good for their employees. They have forgotten that people are not in a single category; that the hot button that makes one person click might be the negative switch that stops another from being productive. The value systems which act as "modes of adjustment" fluctuate within each person. It is even inexact to put any one person into any one value system because as each person moves through life, he will move through some or all of these systems, based on how he copes with his perception of the reality of the world. The Value System Analysis helps personnel officers to avoid putting round pegs (people) into square holes (job).

Value Systems Analysis dates back to the original work of Clare W. Graves, a psychologist at Union College in New York. Graves believes that human beings exist at different "levels of existence" and that both individuals and social systems evolve and regress through these clusters. Thus, an individual operating at a particular predominant level will exhibit the values, beliefs, and behavior that form a consistent package for that level. Graves identifies seven levels or seven value systems. They are as follows:

VALUE SYSTEMS USED IN VSA[1]

Existential

A personal activist who seeks to live within society's constraints while enjoying his maximum individual freedom. Tends to be inner directed and self-motivating. Readily accepts ambiguity in people and situations. This value system is quite tolerant, (7) but, at the same time, expects high levels of performance of itself and others. Responds to reasons, not to rules, and is managed through competence, not status or position. May be expressed by dropping out of society in order to pursue individualistic interests and alternative life-styles.

Manipulative

Achievement-oriented, self-saving, and aggressive—but within the constraints of society. Enjoys wheeling and dealing, engaging in various forms of competition, and demonstrating (5) his ability to motivate, attain goals, and get ahead in life. Manipulation may be either conceded and private or it may be open, aboveboard and displayed. Designed to produce evidence

Sociocentric

Personalistic concern for self discovery, acceptance, human dignity, and the uniqueness of each person, as well as the inherent worth of people as a (6) whole. By finding basic value in people and humanity in general, a sociocentric individual will spend his time and/or energy working in behalf of social causes. Sociocentrics are opposed to the manipulative use of people, as well as the mindless, punitiveness of rigid conformity systems. Reflected in the "helping" professions and new theories and methods of personal introspection.

13

of success, accomplishment, and winning. This mode of adjustment will be found in abundance in politics, management, and in sales and marketing professions.

Egocentric

Unabashed, self-centered assertiveness. Aggressiveness takes many forms as he rebels against authority figures, norms, rules and standards. Somewhat flamboyant behavior in order to gain attention. Often brash, rough, brazen, abrasive and even uncouth. May appear "paranoid" —feels that the world is a hostile and alien place. May internalize the impulses into an angry, embittered and bristling personality. Manifests itself positively in creativity, willingness to break with tradition and dogged determination.

Reactive

Functions at the physiological level—reacts to stimuli such as hunger, pain, cold, warmth, and sleep in order to obtain the immediate satisfaction of basic human needs. Pure Reactives are virtually valueless—concerned only with survival. Seen in new born infants, profoundly retarded, severe stroke victims, and the senile elderly. Can be either a temporary state like a a person on drugs or in a state of emotional or physical shock or a permanent state of existence.

(4)

(3)

(2)

(1)

Conformist

Finds structure, security, and predictability in systems of various types rooted in directive design. Strongly committed to what he considers to be the "right way." Promotes clearly defined social roles—prefers order, structure, patterns, and sequential time frames. Somewhat rigid in responding to diversity, ambiguity. Likes a "cut and dried" kind of world and is proved to impose his system, concepts of right and wrong, rules, and procedures on others. Places a premium on sacrifice, discipline, and adhering to the established norms of society.

Tribalistic

Seeks safety and security in a threatening world by fixating on power, chieftains, clans, rituals, or superstition. Strong reliance on chieftain(s) (parents, teachers, coaches, supervisors, etc.) or the norms established by a clan (family, work unit, team, or tribe). Depends on the mystical forces inherent in life and tends to be both superstitious and ritualistic. Needs to find some way to explain the unexplainable. Expressed in highly visible group affiliation and preference for paternalistic atmospheres.

Value Systems Analysis discovers the *how* of value acquisition. VSA is interested into the *why* questions which search for the value set.

The seven levels are also classified as: *Automatic Existence* (First Subsistence Level); *Tribalistic Existence* (Second Subsistence Level); *Egocentric Existence* (Third Subsistence Level); *Saintly Existence* (Fourth Subsistence Level); *Materialistic Existence* (Fifth Subsistence Level); *Personalistic Existence* (Sixth Subsistence Level); and *Cognitive Existence* (First Being Level), and *Experientialistic Existence* (Second Being Level).

The Philippine-Value-System

If we analyze the Filipino value system based on the theoretical concepts and VSA model of Clare W. Graves the following is the result:

1. *Subsistence Levels*

The first six levels of existence are classified as subsistence levels. The overall goals of these levels are individual survival and dignity. Below are the various levels within the category:

(1) Automatic Existence. Filipino value which is within this level is economic security. At this level the Filipino seeks only the immediate satisfaction of his basic physiological needs. He lives purely on the basis of physiological needs.

(2) Tribalistic Existence. Filipino values which are within this level are: personalistic view of the universe, supernaturalistic world-view, nonscientific and nonrational beliefs, cyclic and psychological time-orientation, *bahala na, suwerte, gaba, awa ng Diyos*. At this level the Filipino defends a life he does not understand. Notwithstanding this, he trusts that his tribal ways are inherent in things. Here is a life based on myth, tradition, and mystical phenomenon full of spirits, magic, and superstition.

(3) Egocentric Existence. Filipino values which are within this level are: *amor propio, hiya, kaulaw, ka-ikog, kataha, tayo-tayo* system, Filipino subservience, ambivalence, noninterference. At this level, the raw, rugged, self-assertive individualism of the Filipino comes to the fore. Both the authoritarian and the submissive develop standards which they feel will insure them against threat.

(4) Saintly Existence. Filipino values within this level are *pagtitiis*, solidarity, *utang-na-loob, bayanihan*, religiosity. At this level, the Filipino perceives that living in this world does not bring

ultimate pleasure. Obedience to God's rule is the price that one must pay for a more lasting life.

(5) Materialistic Existence. Filipino values within this level are economic security, social mobility, *palakasan*, nepotism and relation, Filipino concept of property. At this level, the Filipino strives to conquer the world by learning its secrets. He utilizes objective, positivistic, operationalistic, scientific method to meet his materialistic ends.

(6) Personalistic Existence. Filipino values within this level are social acceptance, *pagsasarili*, acceptance of the person, fear of rejection, sensitivity to personal affront, SIR (Smooth Interpersonal Relations), pleasantness, desire to please and not to hurt, *pakikisama*, euphemism, use of go-between, Filipino hospitality, love for affiliations. At this level, the Filipino becomes concerned with belonging, with being accepted, with knowing his inner self and of others for harmony to result and individuals to be at peace with themselves and with the world.

2. *Being Level*

(7) Cognitive Existence. Filipino values within this level are love for education and self-development, refinement. At this level, the Filipino aspires to be "all he can be and can continue to be." He uses his intellect, acting with all rationality. He uses knowledge to put his world together and in a systematic way.

(8) Experientialistic Existence. Filipino values within this level are family kinship system, *barkada*, grading, and general social class, power, region, language, deep sense of personal worth, self-esteem, love and respect for life. At this level, the Filipino humanness is emphasized. He will do his best to bring balance of nature.

The Filipino Aims, Goals, and Aspirations

Fr. Frank Lynch[2] identifies *social acceptance, economic security,* and *social mobility* as the three basic aims that predominantly motivate and control the behavior of the Filipino. Of the three, he considers social acceptance the most important.

1. *Social Acceptance as a Goal*
Social acceptance is defined as being taken by one's fellow for

what he is or is believed to be and being that image in accordance with his status. Acceptance is especially enjoyed when it includes an outward manifestation of approval that makes clear to the individual that he is liked by those with whom he deals, or is considered important by his superiors. It would be delightful for the employee, for instance, to be given a pat on the back for a job well done.

Fr. Lynch notes, however, that the aim of being accepted is not often conceived of explicitly and deliberately pursued as such. Rather the "desirability of social acceptance is for the model Filipino an implied postulate, but a cultural theme nonetheless."[3]

Attainment of social acceptance is assisted by two intermediate values which are recognized as important and satisfying goals. These are smoothness of interpersonal relations, on the one hand; and sensitivity to personal affront, on the other.

(1) Smooth Interpersonal Relation (SIR). SIR may be defined as "the ability to get along with others in such a way as to avoid outside signs of conflict."[4] The methods used to maintain SIR include pakikisama, euphemisms, and the use of go-between.

a. Pakikisama

This refers to giving in or yielding to the wish of the leader or the majority, even when at times, it contradicts one's ideas or the common good. More than anything else, the Filipino wants to get along well with everyone; he considers it very much necessary to maintain good relations, to feel that he belongs, to be socially accepted. In a field study by Randolf David on the social organization of stevedore groups on the Manila docks,[5] he found out that "pakikisama is a vital concept in the waterfront." As one cabo explains,[6] "there are three kinds of stevedores: those who know their jobs, but cannot get along with others *(hindi marunong makisama)*, those who do not know their jobs but can get along with others *(marunong makisama)*, and those who know their jobs and can also get along with others *(marunong pang makisama)*." Workers of the third category are best, of course, but they are short in supply. The next best is not the stevedore who knows his job, but the one who knows how to get along with others. As the cabo explained, "unskilled stevedores who know how to get along with others can be easily handled because he fits well;

17

however, those who are skilled but cannot get along are hard to handle. They are not worth having in the system."

b. Euphemism

He is defined as the art of stating an unpleasant truth, opinion, or request as pleasantly as possible. "It is an art that has long been highly priced in the Philippine society, and is no less highly regarded today. Harsh and insulting word is correspondingly devalued."[7]

c. The go-between

He serves to prevent a direct confrontation between individuals or groups. He is used to assuage a bruise, heal a wound, or prevent injury. The intermediary is used preventively in a number of common situations: the embarrassing request, complaint, or decision is often communicated through a middleman to avoid the hiya (shame) of a face-to-face encounter.

(2) Sensitivity to Personal Affront. The loss of social acceptance is guarded against two sanctions discouraging behavior descriptive of those relations. First, there is the universal sanction of hiya or shame. The second is amor propio.

a. Hiya

Bulatao defines hiya[8] as a "painful emotion arising from a relationship with an authority figure or with society, inhibiting self-assertions in a situation which is perceived as dangerous to one's ego." It is a fear of being left exposed, unprotected and unaccepted. It is a fear of abandonment, of "loss of soul," a loss not only of one's profession or even of one's life but of something perceived as most valuable than life itself—the ego, the self. Hiya is the universal condition that regulates social behavior. When one violates a norm, he ordinarily feels a deep sense of shame, a realization of having failed to live up to the standards of society.

Because of the fear of being different from others, hiya brings about the employee's conformity or adherence to the company policies and rules.

b. Amor Propio

Amor propio functions to protect the individual against loss of social acceptance or to arouse in him the feeling to regain it, once it has been lost or diminished. It is that sense of self-esteem that prevents a person from swallowing his

18

pride. It is sensitivity to personal insult or affront. Amor propio, however, is not aroused by every insult, slight remark, or offensive gesture. The stimulus that sets it off is only that which strikes at the individual's most highly valued attributes. For example, the average Filipino farmer is not greatly concerned over his inability to read and write; but if he is accused of being an improvident father, his core values and attitudes questioned, his reaction is likely to be violent.

2. *Economic Security*

For the average Filipino, economic security as a goal means the desire to possess the essentials for a decent human life and the opportunities for improving oneself. This implies the economic ability to satisfy one's material needs with the fruits of one's own efforts without borrowing from others. It suggests enough self-sufficiency to maintain one's dignity.

Instrumental to this goal-value of economic security is the value of *reciprocity*. According to Mary R. Hollnsteiner, reciprocity is that principle of behavior wherein every service, solicited or not, demands a return, the nature and proportion of the return determined by the relative statuses of the parties involved and the kind of exchange of issue. In her study she came out with a threefold classification: contractual, quasi contractual and utang na loob.[9]

Contractual reciprocity supposes a voluntary agreement between two or more people to behave toward one another in a specified way for a specified time in the future. Quasi-contractual regulates balanced exchanges where the terms of repayment are not explicitly stated in situations which the culture recognizes and defines as calling for these terms.

Utang na loob reciprocity is most consciously generated when a transfer of goods or services takes place between individuals belonging to two different groups. Since one does not ordinarily expect favors from anyone not in his own group, a service of this kind throws the norm into bold relief. Furthermore, it compels the recipient to show his gratitude by properly returning the favor with interest to be sure that he does not remain in the other person's debt.

Another instrumental value to economic security is *authority value*. This may be defined as "approved by the authority figure and by society, authority's surrogate."[10] This value stresses the unquestioning compliance and even subservience to the leader's decision and goals. There is a fear of stirring up conflict with people who count, thus giving rise to a need for SIR.

A Filipino does not reveal one's thoughts completely to strangers, but only those aspects of one's thought which will be acceptable to them. The fear is that of exposing one's ego to danger. Underlying this value is anxiety for a self-esteem based on group estimation. Attack upon this value is a wound to the amor propio and may result in violent retaliation as when an authority figure fails to recognize a person's merit or treats a person casually.

3. *Social Mobility*

The Filipino seeks social mobility or advancement to a higher social class or position for the improvement of one's lot and one's family, as well as for the enjoyment of accompanying rewards, influence, power, and prestige.

There is the Filipino laborer who works hard to earn a living. He is an industrious worker, always keeping in mind the success and happiness of his children; the wife dreams of her husband eventually becoming successful in business. Their children, on the other hand, prefer to enrol in an exclusive school. It is their greatest desire to be economically stable to be socially recognized.

Filipino Beliefs, Convictions, and Attitudes

The Filipino world-view is personalistic and he explains the physical reality in a religious and metaphysical manner. He looks at the world and nature as controlled by other beings different from himself and governed by forces above him. His fatalism leads him to believe that one's life is shaped and directed by superior forces beyond one's control. He interprets success or failure, health or sickness, life or death, a good or bad harvest on the basis of the supernatural and a trust and reliance on a divine providence. A Filipino student, for example, prays for success in examination but is not interested in reviewing. He carefully follows a *novena* prayer book or rituals but is not inclined to experiment on a new method of learning. This attitude is reflected in his bahala na or *malas* and suwerte mentality. His approach to truth is *intuitive* rather than rational or scientific.

The Filipino conceives success as due more to suwerte, fate, God's mercy or *panalangin*, or the help of others; thus, he considers success as undeserved and can not be claimed entirely for himself but shares it and its fruits with others. Failure is explained in a similar manner. A poor harvest is not due so much to poor irrigation or poor seed, as to bad lack or *gaba*. The Filipino thus learns to submit to uncertainty, to take a bahala na attitude, and to develop traits of resignation, patience, and pagtitiis (endurance). Furthermore, since good is limited, not everyone is expected to enjoy success and happiness at the same time. The Filipino is patient. He believes that there is a time and place for everything and if one is patient, one's time will come.

The Filipino time-orientation is psychological rather than mathematical; cyclic, not linear; relative, not exact. Time is for the person. It fits every happening harmoniously into scheme of life and nature. For the Filipino it is easy to accept any event, because all things come in their own good time.

Filipino Principles and Norms

1. *Structure*

The basic element of the Filipino social structure according to Jocano is *kinship*. He affirms:[11]

It is through this structural unit of society that much local authority, rights and obligation and modes of interactions are expressed, defined, ordered and systematized.

In the Philippine setting, a newborn child is immediately given a status and a position within the group he belongs. At the same time, this status in turn carries with it already defined relations, rights, and position within the society. Whether the group he belongs to is the family or society he is expected to act in accordance with the norms of the kinship. *Structurally* speaking the social system in the Philippines is the kinship system. Philippine society is markedly segmented into subgroups with which the members identify themselves to exclusion of others. The existence of two distinct personal possessive pronouns in Philippine language (*amin, atin, ato, amon, aton*, etc.) compared to only one English

21

term "our" delineates the distinction between the in-group and the out-group. Individual interests are subordinated to those of the in-group; loyalties are strong but limited and particularistic.

The most important and highly valued segment in the Philippine society is the family and the kinship system. Obligations to the family are of the highest order. For the Filipino, the concept "blood is thicker than water" is highly regarded. Within the network of his alliance system which consists of relatives, friends, or followers, status, age-grading, generation, authority and power differentials are ranked and observed.

The Filipino family ordinarily consists of the grandparents, the parents, and the children. The father is the head of the family but while he rules, the mother governs. "For it is the mother that reigns in the home, she is the educator, the financial officer, the laundry woman and the cook."[12] But over and above the "ruler" (husband) and the "governor" or "commander" (as some husbands call the wife) are the grandparents, whose decisions on all important matters are sought. The grandparents are consulted and what they say carries much weight. Ignore them and you risk their stinging rebuke. In cases of medical treatment of a child, when the grandparents say that an *arbulario* (quack doctor) is more competent than a *medico* (medical man or professional doctor), and you wring your hands in sheer frustration because the grandparents would never let a medico touch the sick child, we already see the true weight of grandparents' words and decisions. Such is the "tyranny" of the elders in the Philippines! Respect for the elder is one Filipino value that has remained in the book of unwritten laws. The Filipino parents exercise almost absolute powers over the children. It is unthinkable for a Filipino to do an important thing without consulting his parents. The language of the Filipino denotes deep-seated respect for elders especially in the use of the particle *po*, the use of a second person plural *kayo, inyo*, or *ninyo;* the use of the first person plural *atin, natin, tayo;* and the use of third person plural *sila, nila, kanila.*

Region, language, and religious affiliation also constitute groupings with corresponding ties and allegiances. Pertinent to the structural principles and norms of the Filipino is *ritual kinship.* Introduced as part of the Christian cultures, this ritual was originally thought of to ensure the godchild's *(inaanak)* education in the faith. This kinship is acquired immediately during the Christian's performance of the sacraments such as baptism and confirmation. After such ceremonies, the godparents *(ninong* and *ninang)* immediately become the *compadre* and *comadre* of the parents of the child. The compadre system not only establishes itself between godparents and parents but also among godparents in case of multiple godparents.

In the official Catholic laws, no statement is mentioned about the spiritual relationship between witnesses and the bridal pair, but the Filipino ingenuity has transformed this sacrament as another source of compadre system.[13] The bridal pair becomes the inaanak and the godparents and parents establish the compadre system among themselves.

In the Philippine setting, the ninong usually comes from the upper income group, the social and political elite of the society. This has become a means of establishing rapport between people of different status, by incorporating non-family members into the kinship-realm of a Filipino. The usage of the compadre system in the Philippines is in fact of big magnitude and clearly exploitative. This practice is easily seen in the political, private, and business organizations. A political candidate campaigning for votes in a remote community would always be willing to stand in baptism, confirmation, and matrimony to act as ninong, pose for pictures, then go to other communities to perform the same act again because come election day, the compadre and comadre will dutifully elect them. The usage of the compadre system in the private sectors has come to mean job granting, money in times of need, the lending of one's transportation vehicles, and medical attendance. In business entities, numerous employees are promoted on the basis of compadre system alone although nobody can prove the fact.

Another Filipino structural principle is *regionalism* which is defined as a tendency to emphasize and value, oftentimes to extremes, the qualities and characteristics of life in a particular region. The Filipino is regionalistic and he thinks only in terms of regional oneness instead of national boundaries. As Agoncillo and Alfonso put it:[14]

Regionalism is an extension of the closeness of family ties. Invariably, the Filipino believes that the person known to him, no matter how bad is better than the one unknown to him.

Philippine history clearly marks regionalism as an important factor in the events that happened centuries ago. Regionalism can be traced back to the Spanish colonial policy of "divide and conquer." During this time, the Spanish administrators recognizing regionalism in the Filipinos, made use of the latter to prevent consolidation of a national revolution and to put down numerous revolts. The effectiveness of a national revolution waited for more than three centuries to be recognized because regionalism showed itself in the minor revolts in different regions of Ilocos, Cebu, Bulacan, and others. Carried to the extent, the regionalistic trait was even used by Spanish authorities to make Filipinos fight Filipinos (e.g. the Tagalog Revolt put down by the Pampangos, the Pampango Revolt put down by the Ilocanos, and vice versa).

The phenomenon of regionalism is present today such as in the case when a Filipino is confronted with insurmountable odds in a totally alien city, his general tendency is to seek the support, protection, or merely the comfort of a provincial or national *kababayan*. As Gorospe would say it:[15]

> Regionalism, a trait a migrant had substituted for independence and self-sufficiency, re-surfaces as he is confronted with the problems of the strange and complex city. He seeks his fellow migrants especially his "kababayan."

Filipinos have the natural tendency to band together segregating themselves according to regions and hometowns. Social status, sex, age, and other differences seem to break their barriers at the mention of *magkababayan* and a closer interpersonal relationship, carried almost to the degree of kinship, is expected mutually of both parties at this point of time.

2. Operational

Equivalence and *solidarity* refer to how the segments are viewed by the members of a group and by those not belonging to it. Individual members are equated with the whole total group membership in a family gathering or a social affair. Co-members look at themselves as united into a solid group against other groups. Thus, a kindness or an injury done to one member of the group applies to all the group members. The success of one is the honor of all; the disgrace of one embarrasses the other members as well.

Utang na loob is a feeling of indebtedness which is incurred when one receives a favor, service or good, and a deep sense of

24

obligation to reciprocate when the appropriate moment comes. It is that principle of behavior wherein service received, solicited or not, demands a return; and proposition of the return determined by the relative statuses of the parties involved and the kind of exchange called for. A cultural example would be the *bolhon* (cooperation) practice in the Visayan region where farmers in a certain locality work together to till the land of another farmer, the latter acting as boss because the land being tilled at the moment is his. When it becomes the turn of another farmer, the former boss now becomes a worker for him. Another example is the traditional custom of *abuloy* which is given to the family of the one who died. The members of the family then note the people who gave for future reciprocity in the same form in case of deaths in the family of these people. Some instances when utang na loob arises are when professional services are rendered and no fee is charged. Utang na loob is also incurred when the debtor is financially hard-up, when politicians pull strong to secure a job for a non-qualified godson or distant relative, or when a person sends a friend's child to school.

Within the Filipino family, parents expect their children to be forever grateful to their parents; their utang na loob to them should be immeasurable and eternal, unlike in the West where parents regard it as their duty to raise their children with nothing expected in return. Thus the Filipino is practically at the mercy of his "creditor." Sooner or later, some form of payment will have to be made in partial fulfillment of the eternal obligation.

Awa, kaluoy or compassion is another operational principle and norm of the Filipino. It is a sentiment of sympathy, mercy, or pity aroused when someone suffers misfortune or injustice. It is the willingness to be identified with the victim of fate or human cruelty. An individual is appreciated for his refined sense of gratitude, thoughtfulness and concern, solicitude and consideration for another's needs and feelings. Awa is supplication, compassion, plea for mercy.

Awa used in the name of charity, goodwill, justice, humane treatment, family emergencies, human relations, and fair play seeps into practically every phase of Filipino life. A job applicant who has very limited qualifications or who has none at all applies for a job in the name of awa. A sweepstake vendor approaches a churchgoer and sells her ticket in the name of awa. An employee caught stealing company property pleas for awa. A friend or relative approaches a well-to-do relative to borrow money not on the basis of the four C's of credit but in the name of awa. The person or official who denies the pleas or requests made to him is branded as *walang-puso* (without heart), hindi marunong makisama (anti-social), *walang kuwentang tao* (worthless person).

Personalism, another Filipino operational principle, attaches major importance to the personal factor which guarantees intimacy, warmth, and security of kinship and friendship in getting things done. This value can be the foundation of genuine commitment, authentic respect for the human person, meaningful involvement, deep loyalty, and mature freedom. However, the Filipino way of doing things is centered very much on personalities. To get results, a Filipino manager has to get in touch personally with an employee or fellow-official either by meeting him personally or by phone before or after he sends him a memo. Thus it is very difficult for a Filipino to dissociate personalities making it hard for him to be really objective in making judgments. Lack of trust between contracting parties and the mobility to exchange the best possible service and goals exist in any transaction if the *kilala* (personal reference) system has not been tapped. There is short-lived enthusiasm for the support and maintenance of organization outside kinship and friendship circles. The Filipino cannot easily understand that while it is true that personal worth is in the final analysis what a person is, what he does, his behavior and performance, his merit more than his status, prove his real worth. Palakasan emphasizes status-differentials and leads to abuse and exploitation of the weak by the strong *(ang malakas)*. Palakasan is the Filipino version of the spoils system whereby the booty (which may consist of privileges, benefits, and other material or financial profits) is given to or divided among members, allies, or friends of the clique in power. This is the testing of the powers of one's in-group as against competing groups. This obviously is the antithesis of the merit system, because, through palakasan, a person inferior in ability, competence, or attainment can manage to get hold of a position to which there are more deserving candidates.

Pagsasarili means the burning ambition of every Filipino to be self-reliant, to be himself, to be a person in his own right, to make up his own mind, to do his thing. This principle is deeply rooted in his national tradition. The high evaluation Filipinos place on it may have been conditioned by their colonial experience.

THE PHILIPPINE-VALUE SYSTEM[16]
(Lynch, Bulatao, Gorospe, Hollnsteiner,
Landa Jocano, Mercado, Quisumbing)

Aims, Goals and Aspirations	Belief, Convictions & Attitudes	Principles and Norms
A. Social Acceptance	A. Personalistic view of the universe	A. Structural
		1. Segmentation
P Acceptance of the **S** Person	Supernaturalistic **P** world-view **A**	family kinship system
E (fear of rejection, sensitivity to personal affront) **R S O N A L I S M**	Non-Scientific, Non-Rational **R T I C U L A R I S M**	age-grading and generation social class power region language religion
P	B. Perception of Reality	
E	non-dualistic	
R	harmonizing	
N SIR	interpersonal	
A Pleasantness	concrete,	2. Ranking
T (desire to	elaborate	vertical
U please, not	poetic, artistic,	horizontal
R to hurt)	intuitive	B. Operational
A *pakikisama*	C. Time-Orientation	1. Equivalence
L euphemism	cyclic, not linear	2. Solidarity
I use of go-	psychological,	3. Reciprocity
S between	not mathemat-	*utang-na-loob*
M	ical	4. Compassion
B. Economic Security	D. Good is Limited	*awa, kaluoy*
C. Social Mobility	E. Success or Failure is underserved *bahala na, suwerte, gaba, awa ng Diyos*	5. Non-interference

Value Themes

A. Emotional Closeness and Security in the FAMILY

B. Approval by AUTHORITY

C. Economic and Social Betterment

D. Patience, Endurance, Suffering

HIYA
kaulaw
ka-ikog
kataha

Social Sanctions:

AMOR PROPIO
deep sense of
personal worth
self-esteem

with PEOPLE   with NATURE

HARMONY

Filipino Value System Analysis: Implications to Management

Filipino Value System Analysis can be applied as a diagnostic, preventive, and therapeutic tool in a large number of areas ranging from the management of the home to the recruitment of new employees; the selection and assessment of potential managers; training and developing teachers, students, parents, married couples, and organizations. This is a method that can help individuals solve problems, cope with problems, and cope with their environment.

Filipino Value System Analysis provides management with a new framework for understanding human behavior. A manager knows that each subordinate under him is different. He is different because of his value system. The manager must know how to analyze his workers' value system. By applying the Filipino Value System Analysis, management can make the employees' function more responsively to the objectives of the company, while at the same time making themselves responsible to their employees. In truth and in fact, management cannot impose its values on the employees nor the employees their values on management. However, we know through the Filipino Value System Analysis that one person does not stay within just one of the value systems delineated; he passes from one system to another as the conditions within his living environment change. Thus management will know what to do or stress to each individual worker according to his level. Take for example an employee who is in Level 5 (Achievist), personal career advancement opportunities should be stressed. On the other hand, we need to emphasize the individual advantages of performance for an employee who is in Level 3 (Egocentric).

Filipino Value System Analysis can also be applied to personnel functions such as in actual job placements. What is the value system of an applicant? Let's say you need an employee or officer for a long-range plan. It will be dangerous to get an employee for the position who is in Level 2 (Tribalistic), for whom day-to-day performance is only what matters. It helps personnel staff to know where people come from, how they operate, what makes them tick.

Implications to Job Performance

Filipino Value System Analysis helps in behavior modification

Motivational System	Problem of Existence	Means Values	End Values	Learning System
iodic hysiological eeds (e.g., unger)	Maintaining physiological stability	No conscious value system Values are purely reactive	No conscious value system Values are purely reactive	Habituation (The individual adapts to his environment by a process of becoming accustomed to certain things.)
surance iodic hysiological eeds (e.g., varmth)	Achievement of relative safety	Traditionalism Suwerte-Malas Supernaturalism Filipino time Superstitiousness, rituals	Safety bahala na Optimistic fatalism	Classical Conditioning (The individual learns through the association of one thing with another.)
ysiological urvival	Living with self-awareness	Exploitation subservience ambivalence, nepotism, noninterference, compadre system, palakasan	Power amor propio hiya	Operant Conditioning (People learn best when they are rewarded for learning tasks.)
curity der aning	Achieving everlasting peace of mind	Sacrifice pagtitiis utang na loob religiousness	Salvation Pagkabayani Life after death	Avoidant Learning (People learn when they are punished for errors.)
lependence equacy mpetency	Conquering the physical universe	Scientism love for education intuitiveness	Materialism pagmamayari sense of property	Expectancy (One learns best when the outcome of their behavior meets their expectation. They learn through own efforts.)

Continued

Level of Existence	Thinking	Characteristics	Examples
6. Sixth Subsistence Level	Relativistic (Things depend on particular situation) Sociocentric Personalistic	People-oriented Humanness	HRD managers
7. First Being Level	Systematic Individualistic Cognitive	Freedom lover Highly self-motivated and inner directed	activists revolutionists
8. Second Being Level	Differential Synergistic Experientialistic	Partnership Listening to others	business partners

Level of Existence	Thinking	Characteristics	Examples	
First Subsistence Level	Automatic Reactive	Survival-oriented	newborn babies severely retarded severe stroke victims elderly senile	Pe p n h
Second Subsistence Level	Autistic Tribalistic	Clannish, Supertitious, Authority- follower		As Pe p ʏ ᵥ
. Third Subsistence Level	Egocentric	Self-centered Assertive to the point of aggres- siveness Thirsty for power	sales people	Ph s
. Fourth Subsistence Level	Absolutistic (Thinking in term of dogmas, rules) Saintly	Conformist Structure-oriented Straight forward- ness	accounting people bureaucrats	Se Or Me
. Fifth Subsistence Level	Multiplistic Achievist Materialistic	Go-getters Wheels-dealers goal setters and reachers Competitive type	corporate executives	In Ac Cc

Motivational System	Problem of Existence	Means Values	End Values	Learning System
Affiliation level	Living with the human element	Sociocentricity Filipino hospitality, personalism, familism hiya amor propio	Community bayanihan Nationalism Internationalism	*Observational* (People learn by watching other people and serving how they act. Learning through vicarious experience.)
Existence Self-worth	Restoring viability to a disordered world	Accepting pagsasarili titulado	Existence Status-Consciousness	Since people at the 7th and 8th levels are in the second ladder of existence and all basic syste
Experience ? ? ? ? ?	Accepting existential dichotomies	Experiencing love and respect for life	Communion, union with God and fellowmen	are more open, learning in any fo can and does take place.

such as improving job performance. It helps management understand why others behave the way they do. Understanding behavior is an important prerequisite to influencing behavior. Each worker brings to his job certain likes, dislikes, and personality traits which make up his "value sets." When these value sets conflict with those in his job, then the job suffers. This conflict results in poor work attitude, absenteeism, tardiness, low productivity, and general discontentment for the worker as well as for those around him. If we apply Filipino Value System Analysis, we should analyze the job to be filled up to find out the characteristics required for its successful completion.

Different jobs require different value sets for success. Corporate executives, for example, are in Level 5 (Achievist) since they are goal setters and reachers. Marketing people are in Level 3 (Egocentric) since their thirst for power and self-centeredness make them assertive. Finance people who pay close attention to detail are in Level 4 (Absolutistic) since they must conform, are structure-oriented, and do things in "the right way." Human resource people are in Level 6 (Sociocentric) since they are people-oriented who see value in the individual rather than in material things. They like to help other people and humanity in general. Business partners are in Level 8 (Synergistic) since they work effectively with others.

To apply Filipino Value System Analysis in personnel functions, the value sets as criteria for the jobs must be clear. These value sets must be internalized so that objectivity can be practised in selecting people, with knowledge and skill to generate behavior from the applicant to ascertain his value sets.

Workers normally prefer to be managed by the style congruent with his level of existence. People who are at Level 3 (Egocentric) to be productive must be managed in a special way. Since his main motivation is survival, management must see to it that his immediate survival needs are secure. Employees who are at Level 7 (Individualistic) must be handled in another way. These are people who want freedom to do their jobs the best way they know. He reacts negatively when demanded to ask approval for everything he does but he reacts positively when he can inform management what he needs to do a job. Every individual develops through a series of levels or behavioral states. At each level, the individual learns and acts in a way that is consonant to that particular level.

31

REFERENCE NOTES

1Based on the theoretical concepts of Clare W. Graves, Union College, New York, and adapted by the Center for Values Research, Box 5156 NTSU Station, Denton, Texas 76203.

2Frank Lynch, "Social Acceptance Reconsidered," *Four Readings on Philippine Values,* ed. Alfonso de Guzman II and Frank Lynch (1976), pp. 1-88.

3Ibid., p. 9.

4Ibid., p. 10.

5Randolf S. David, "Human Relations on the Waterfront: the Cabo System," *Philippine Sociological Review,* Vol. 15, Nos. 3 and 4, p. 135.

6Ibid., p. 138.

7Lynch, p. 11.

8Jaime C. Bulatao, "Hiya," *Philippine Studies,* Vol. 12 (1964), p. 428.

9Mary R. Hollnsteiner, "Reciprocity in the Lowland Philippines," *Philippine Studies* (1976), p. 69.

10Jaime Bulatao, "The Manileno's Mainspring," *Four Readings on Philippine Values,* ed. Alfonso de Guzman II and Frank Lynch (1976), p. 102.

11F. Landa Jocano, "Filipino Social Structure and Value System," *Management of Men,* ed. J.B.M. Kassaryian and Robert A. Stringer, Jr. (1971), p. 410.

12Teodoro Agoncillo and Oscar Alfonso, *A Short History of the Filipino People* (University of the Philippines, 1961), p. 7.

13Mary R. Hollnsteiner et al., *Society, Culture and the Filipino,* Trial Edition, Vol. 1, 1975, p. 95.

14Agoncillo and Alfonso, *History of the Filipino People,* p. 9.

15Vitaliano R. Gorospe and Richard L. Deats, *The Filipino in the Seventies,* An Ecumenical Perspective (Quezon City: New Day Publishers, 1973), p. 65.

16Handout distributed during the 16th Annual Convention of the Psychological Association of the Philippines, October 11-13, 1979.

17Clara S. Graves, "Human Nature Prepares for a Momentous Leap," *The Futurist* (April, 1974), pp. 72-78.

Management by Values

3

Management is generally defined as the achievement of objectives through people. Management in the Philippines started in tribes and barangays. Before the coming of the Spaniards, barangays were small absolute monarchies confined within large families bound by the common value of material protection. Each barangay had a leader or a *datu*, frequently at war with each other because of conflict of values over lands, rights, possessions, and duties.

History has made the Filipino a man of many values. He integrates the rich Christian values of Europe; the pragmatic and democratic values of America, signified by the dollar and the ballot; and also the pride, poverty, and spiritual values of Asia.

There is, therefore, a need to examine very critically our values to discover our management potentials and weaknesses so that from such a study we may be able to draw out the blueprint for the Filipino manager. There should be an examination of Filipino values whether they be cultural, utilitarian, humanistic, pragmatic, materialistic, or sentimental.

Many organizations which have introduced a management system during the last few years have found that it just did not work satisfactorily for them. Perhaps Management By Values would provide the answer.

Management By Values Defined

Management By Values (M.B.V.) is a planning and result-oriented strategy wherein management clarifies its value-goals to employees or participants who simultaneously are given the opportunity to clarify their personal values and to examine whether these are compatible with those of management. In its simplest form, it is harmonizing individual's personal values with the management's values toward the achievement of the most appropriate and mutually internalized values.

M.B.V. is founded on the value clarification theory. Value clarification is based on the belief that human beings hold the possibility of being thoughtful and wise. It affirms that the most appropriate values surface when persons use their intelligence freely and reflectively to define their values and relationships with each other and with an ever-changing world. As the world changes, as man changes, and as man strives to change his world, he has many decisions to make and he should be learning how to make these decisions. He should be learning *how to value.* M.B.V. gives emphasis on the value system of all the members of an organization or company. It stresses the fact that before any management system should be implemented, each and every implementor of the system must see to it that his values are clarified and harmonized with the goal-values.

Management By Values System

1. Considers Filipino values as potentials for effective organization and productivity.
2. Builds skills and confidence in supervisors and managers that enable them to successfully harness Filipino values toward company commitment, high productivity, and efficiency.
3. Assures the effective compatibility between management's values and employee's values.
4. Meets specific training needs because of its internalization and positive orientation and redirection of values in which motivation and competence are premised.
5. Trains managers and supervisors to effectively reinforce creativity, management, and zeal through value clarification and value-conflict resolution.

Value Clarification Processes

There are three processes of valuing:

First Process: *Choosing Values.* The mainspring of human behavior is the will. The will is the faculty which acts with reflection and freedom. It is the faculty which decides the course of action after deliberation. The will expresses itself in choices which presuppose freedom or full possession of one's self. Thus, *values must be freely chosen.*

However, choice must be preceded by deliberation wherein one examines and weighs the different courses of action or values. There is no real choice if it is limited to one. Thus, *values must be chosen from among alternatives.*

In deliberation, man must examine the pros and cons of the act or motives, of whatever kind, that solicit the will. The nature of the act or value, its importance and consequences, must be taken into consideration. Thus, *values must be chosen after consideration of each alternative's consequences.* A value can only emerge after one has clearly understood what each alternative will result in.

Second Process: *Prizing Values.* One must *prize and cherish* the values or acts he has chosen. Furthermore, if one has gone through the process of establishing his values he must be *willing to publicly affirm his values* in his desire to share those which he holds for strongly. Value clarification engenders productivity, for man will work for the values which he truly prizes and cherishes.

Third Process: *Acting on Values.* The zenith of values clarification is *acting on one's prized and cherished values.* After man has clarified his values he will begin to apply his new knowledge. He will act with *pattern and consistency, and repeatedly on his values.*

As we can see evidently, the value clarification processes involve both the cognitive domain of human activity as well as the affective domain. When man is asked to make a choice, to decide thoughtfully from alternatives, to analyze an issue and decide, he is asked to think. When he is asked, on the other hand, how he feels about that choice—does he cherish it or is he glad that he made it?—he is asked to consider his affective side. Thus, a value is a result of *both* the affective and cognitive domains. This process gives him pleasure because it accomplishes his development as a person.

Primary and Secondary Values

One of the major concepts in value clarification theory is that of *primary* and *secondary values*. Value clarification as a methodology creates the opportunity for people to discover their own values. The goal is to make aware of what their value indicators demonstrate as their full or partial values according to the criteria. One of the criteria is that the value facilitates the growth of the person and helps him develop his potential. Modern developmental psychology seems to indicate that there are two primary values that most would accept: the value of one's *own* worth and the value of the worth of *others*.

By *primary values* we mean values that are chosen, acted upon, a person is happy with, and are necessary for the authentic development of man. It develops a human being to the best of his capacity and, as such, is motivated to exceptionally function in society. It is basic and as such necessary for development to take place.

Obligatory values are what we call *secondary values*. While it is true that there exists a wide range of values which each person may freely choose from, every society has certain values which all its members must uphold. Through long experience and practice, organizations have determined values which are consistently necessary for the well-being of their members.

Value Indicator

Another important concept of value clarification is that of *value indicator*. A value indicator is simply something which does not meet all criteria and therefore, not a full value. However, a value indicator is important because it shows a person what values he is in the process of forming. He may have a goal but if he is not working toward it, it is not a full value. A worker may have an attitude that he absorbed from his supervisor but which he is not working on. He may say he has an interest in something but does not take the time to act on the interest. Feelings, beliefs, and aspirations are usually value indicators because they do not fulfill all criteria of a full value.

Base and Scope

Akin to value indicators are the concepts of *base* and *scope*. What values does man seek and what technique and values is he using to achieve his sought values? Take for example a working student who works as a gasoline boy to earn some money. His base value is *wealth* (money). However, his intentions are to use the money he is earning to study. Therefore, his scope value is *enlightenment* (studies). It is very important to identify the scope value from the base value, for only in this way can we address ourselves to the underlying causes and basic needs rather than the surface symptoms.

Value Clarification as Applied in Management

Management combines technology and humanity to achieve corporate goals. In truth and in fact, many obstacles to the achievement of corporate goals come not from technology but from the world of people. In management, the world of people must be the first concern before we deal with the world of things. The efficient relationship between people must come first before we talk of the productive relationship of man and machine. This is where value clarification can play an important role.

Value clarification is an approach by which each one in the organization clarifies one's values as the means of building a trusting, creative atmosphere and group spirit conducive to the attainment of corporate objectives. There are several management areas wherein value clarification can be helpful.

1. *Company Goal-Setting*

In many organizations, top management assigns goals for subordinates to achieve without finding out what the latter's values are or if these goals are in harmony with the subordinates' values. Value clarification can be used to find out what the subordinates' values are so that management can approximate their expectations. By this approach, different values and interests surface, and from there, the management could see which ones could work together. Collaborative effort can be achieved only after values are clarified.

2. Human Resource Management

An effective human resource management requires compatibility between position/job assignment and employee's capability. This can be done only if an organization or company clearly knows what its value-goals are. Similarly, personnel recruitment could be done along the standards of these values so that job applicants of similar values could be hired. People with the same value will find it easier to work together. Furthermore, the possibility of staying longer in one company is stronger if the employee has the same value as that of management. For example, in big American corporations geographic mobility is usually a requirement for organizational promotion. A Filipino who holds as a value the dictates of an extended family system may not likely feel at home in such corporations. In human resource development and training, it is management's task to discover what makes employees work and what makes them work harder. This can be done only if we know what their values are. Development and training programs for different levels should be in accordance with their value system. A subordinate could be asked to internalize a system of management only if it is reconciled with his values.

3. Management Problem-Solving and Decision-Making

Problems are no more than conflicts of values. The *situation* is the constituent element in a conflict; that is, even when one value and another value do not antagonize each other since the concrete situation brings it about, only one can be fulfilled and the other must be violated. Take for example the situation in which management places profit above workers' benefit in a company.

Conflict also arises from polarity, a situation in which two groups of people are trying to impose their values upon each other. This happens when management imposes maximization of profit and minimization of expenses as a value to the workers or unions whose values are higher salary, more fringe benefits and leisure hours. Such an imposition of values is a *value ranking situation*. When the persons working together have a consensus in most major areas of management as far as the core values are concerned, the phenomena of conflict and polarity are less frequent.

Filipino Values and Management Practice in the Philippines

The role, tasks, and responsibilities of management do not actually vary, to a significant extent, among organizations; instead, it is the manager/supervisor—with his own unique sets of attitudes and norms—and the kind of subordinates he handles that differ widely in all organizations. To this effect, it becomes necessary to deal with the manager and his subordinates as belonging to a peculiar culture and society which is distinctly Filipino. Thus, the need to deal with the Filipino manager vis-a-vis the Filipino worker in the light of the value systems and attitudes predominant in the Filipino society.

The Filipino Manager/Supervisor

A supervisor is an individual in the organization who directs the activities of the line workers at the lowest level of the organizational hierarchy. In a large organization, the top manager is responsible for setting up the company's objectives, which are generally achieved through the summation of contributions of the bottom level workers and other people connected with that organization. Top management does not usually and it need not directly supervise the tasks of the lowest line workers and it need not directly know the details of their job. This function belongs to the supervisor.

What is the supervisor's role? Some have emphasized that he is a key man in the organization; others say that he is just another worker; still there are propositions that advance the claim that the supervisor is the "man in the middle," the human relations specialist and the "marginal man." Each theory, however, applies only to some organizations hence undermining its generality. The position of the supervisor is critical in the organizational profile because it provides a point of contact between management and workers. Without him, the organization is lacking and crippled, hence, ineffective in achieving its objectives.

The supervisor, being a representative of management and, at the same time, a representative of the workers, is loaded with a paramount of responsibilities. And what are these? First of all, he is responsible for making his men willing and capable to do their work. He is also responsible for setting the objectives of his unit or section, for the development of every single man's performance and for developing future organization needs.[1]

The responsibilities of the supervisor, being numerous and diverse, imply also numerous and diverse tasks. Generally, he directs the work of his subordinates and coordinates their activities through effective communication. In short, he has to manage the workers at the bottom level of the organization. He has to get results—turn out production, maintain quality, hold costs down, keep his employers satisfied—under a set of technical conditions, social relations, and logical abstractions. To do this, he has to see to it that:[2]

(1) schedules are made and adhered to so that the work (of his unit or section) flows evenly and steadily;
(2) the workers or his subordinates have the equipment to do their work;
(3) they have the proper environment conducive for work; and
(4) they have an organized team of fellow workers.

In brief, the supervisor has to synchronize the tasks of his unit with that of the organization's objectives.

With all the responsibilities and work his position entails, the supervisor needs the support from both his superiors and his subordinates. His needs emanating from his superiors are:[3]

(1) clear-cut objectives for his own activity focused directly on the objectives of his company;
(2) authority that goes with the responsibility for reaching his objectives;
(3) knowledge about the company operations, structure, and

goals in relation to his objectives;
(4) adequate promotional opportunities; and
(5) managerial status.

From his subordinates, he needs:

(1) support;
(2) acceptance;
(3) recognition;
(4) respect; and
(5) compliance.

The pattern on which today's Filipino management-worker relation is based dates back to the traditional dyads in early years in the Philippines where there were *datus* and *sakop*, landlords and tenants, owners and slaves, parents and children, *principales* and common *tao*. [4] In all of these superior-inferior relations, there is no middleman to whom authority is delegated because the correspondence is one-to-one. The authority is exercised by the superior face to face and he has the general right to make demands of his inferior involving anything within the sphere of their relation; on the other hand, the inferior can expect any kind of assistance in an equally blanket manner from his superior. It is true that the typical *encargado* in haciendas has been delegated authority; nonetheless, it is his to use or abuse. Thus, the Filipino traditional concept of superior-inferior relations and the modern notion of the middleman in factories and offices do not match each other perfectly. They must both undergo modification in the Philippine setting.

According to a study made by Ernesto A. Franco, present Filipino managers have six origins: (1) *mga anak ng may-ari* or from the traditional families already in business; (2) graduates of the school of hard knocks or self-made entrepreneurs; (3) professionals like lawyers and doctors who strike out on their own; (4) those who come from existing companies or institutions; (5) former public servants or government officials who retire or resign from public service; and (6) MA and PhD degree holders or graduates from the business and management training schools. [5] From observations, we can classify managers in the Philippines into two kinds: (1) the MBA who is a professional manager and a Master of Business Administration, and (2) the MBA, who is an amateur and a 'Manager By Accident.'

Franco enumerates four styles of *Pinoy* (Filipino) Management practiced in the Philippines:[6]

1. the realist-manager who practices Management-by-*Kayod* (or working hard like an ant), that is, he works day in and day out, fired by an inner zeal;
2. the idealist-manager who practices Management-by-*Libro*, that is he prefers American type management styles with technical jargon and all the sophisticated tools of management;
3. the opportunist-manager who practices Management-by-*Lusot* (short-cut or rule-breaking), that is, he works with least hardship and sweat, paying off problems and taking short-cuts;
4. the reconsider-manager who practices Management-by-*Suyod* (suyod is a comb to take away lice from the hair), that is, he looks at the problems at all and every angle, way deep.

The characteristics of a Manager-by-Kayod are: acts fast, autocratic, *sigurista*, first things first, *may oido* (has talent), *kayod nang kayod* (hardworking), knows how to utilize men and resources, cuts problems down to manageable size, decisive, *apurado* (he cannot wait), and *tuso* (wise in a shrewd way). The characteristics of the Manager-by-Libro are: *palaisip* (reflective technocratic), *mabusisi* (detail conscious), *mahilig* (very planning-oriented), *may sistema* (systematic), professional performer, *mabagal* (holistic), thinks carefully before deciding, *matigas ang ulo* (has definite way of working), *mataas ang panaginip* (has lofty ideas), and seeks quality results. The characteristics of the Manager-by-Lusot are: *galawgaw* (vacillating), *walang konsensiya* (unethical), *mahilig sa lusot* (idealmaker), *mahilig sa ayusan* (compromiser), *ayaw ng sakit ng ulo* (passes on the buck), *kung walang atik, walang gawa* or *mahilig sa lagay* (money-oriented). The characteristics of the Manager-by-Suyod are: *may balance* or realistic, knows the strengths and limitations of different management styles, solid, *marunong pumili* or human resource developer, *tatlong mata* or forecaster, and *pambihira* or exceptionally gifted.

In addition to Franco's four styles of Pinoy management, I am adding five more as per experience and observations in private, business, government, education, and ecclesiastical organizations. The first type is Management by *Pakiramdam*. In English, pakiramdam means feeling. It simply means working according to what one feels is the desire of management. He follows exactly what management wants him to do; no more, no less. He follows the

"Golden Rule." The "Rule" is "Management" because **Management** has the "Gold." He has personal loyalty to the people in management. The characteristics of a Manager by Pakiramdam are rule-oriented rather than result-oriented, uncreative, uninnovative, conservative, sheer-follower, dependent, and no decision of his own. He does not even deliberate nor indulge in sophisticated problem-solving nor decision-making; these are for him, useless intellectual gymnastics and mere indulgent in psychic exercise.

The second type is Management by *Takutan* or *Sindakan*. In English, *takot* means "fear." It simply means achieving results by threatening or by inflicting fear. This kind of manager sees to it that his subordinates fear him, his fellow managers fear him, that everybody fears him. He is the nonchalant type; always secretive and aloof. He is uncommunicative. The characteristics of a Manager by Takutan are coerciveness, arrogance, use of threats and punishment, and hostility. He is a slave-driver, dictatorial, and despotic. His motto is "do as told" or *marunong ka pa sa akin*. In meetings, he suppresses questions and objections; he forces his side in all issues.

The third type is Management by *Kulit*. Kulit means in English, following-up or much bother or ado about something. This manager is really communicative in all respects. He follows up things requiring approval of management, he follows up things he has ordered his people to do. He sees to it that every assigned task is well monitored and programmed. He sees to it that there is a person responsible and accountable for every assignment to be done. He interferes in everything which is under his command. He demands religious attention to one's job. He oversees everything assigned to him.

The fourth type is Management by *Patsamba-tsamba*. Patsamba-tsamba in English means "guesswork." This simply means that one works without any direction nor procedure. He is there because he happens to be there as a manager. If he has a system, it is the *kapa-kapa* system; he tries the trial-and-error method in everything he does. His favorite song in everything he does is "Where do I begin."

Evolution of the Filipino Supervisor/Manager*

The Filipino supervisor of this epoch is certainly of a different breed. A product of so many years of evolution, he is less of brawn and more of brains. He is more likely to be creative and ambitious rather than tradition-bound and complacent, management-minded rather than bull-headed like a drill sergeant.

One of his predecessors was the *cabo*, that ugly Spanish creation—a minor despot who usually bidded to provide labor and hired his own gang of workers on whom he made a living. We do not see much of the cabo nowadays, although we see vestiges of him at the piers, airports, and railroad stations among the stevedores. One easily recognizes him as a brawny, tight-lipped, cigar-smoking hulk of a man. He is the combined gang leader and sergeant major that we find on the drill grounds. He is also referred to as the *kapetera* (kettle) type of supervisor, with his two hands always on his waist. A presidential decree under the New Society outlawed the cabo system.

The *capataz* is a Spanish-American hybrid. In the government service we usually find him head of a gang of road construction workers. He is often preoccupied with *dama* games and obsessed with the desire to strut around in a white shirt. This type is also seen supervising private building constructions. He is also referred to as the *po-re-man* (foreman). He is less of an entrepreneur than the cabo. The capataz may have acquired his status because of skill or education and probably by knowing what strings to pull. The foreman most likely started as a carpenter, became a master carpenter, learned masonry, painting, plumbing, and electrical work.

The *superbisor* was a term applied to the school official who visited the schools now and then to see that the "subjects" he was in charge of were properly taught. He worked with the principal and held the ordinary classroom teacher in fear of him. The *hepe* is a term commonly applied to white-collar supervisors.

The supervisor, as used today, is a relatively new title applied to the same position but connoting a different meaning. It refers to a more sophisticated frontline "manager." His job has been enlarged to give emphasis to planning, organizing, directing, and controlling his group's activities.

---

*Esdras Martinez, *Supervisory Development: Text and Cases* (Manila: GIC Enterprises, 1973), p. 2.

The Filipino Worker

The work of the bottom level employee is dependent on the organizational setup but generally, it involves the utilization of his physical skills and abilities. He is mainly responsible for his own contribution. Simple as it may seem, however, it demands horizontal movement or opportunities for advancement, financial incentives, and recognition.

The Filipino worker as an individual, having his own set of values and attitudes, demands more than mere supervision and simple motivation. In specific terms, he requires a certain quality of supervision and motivation that could be assessed in consideration of the value system he lives by.

The value concepts that are predominant in the Filipino culture and relevant to the Filipino worker within the organizational matrix are *hiya* or an emotion-laden attitude involving honor, dignity, and pride; *amor propio* (self-esteem) or the heightened emotional state of hiya; *utang-ng-loob* or the principle of reciprocity; *bata-bata* which means "protege"and carries some functional rights; *pakikisama* or the tendency to level with someone who is out of line and the curbing of anti-social attitudes by disallowing privacy; *pilosopo* which undermines the person who questions prevailing ideas or norms; and *paternalism* which implies a deep respect for elders in consideration of age.

The concepts described above depict the predominant values of the Filipino individual. These values give rise to a particular set of attitudes that the Filipino worker manifests in all his undertakings. The more conspicuous attitudes attendant to the mentioned values are:

(1) the tendency to cooperate without hesitation;
(2) being sensitive and conservative;
(3) the tendency to be obsequiously accommodating and hospitable; and
(4) the respect of elders.

These attitudes are necessary and indispensable to the organization; however, care should be given in dealing with them because the Filipino, as both worker and individual, has a tendency to overemphasize these attitudes. These Filipino attitudes can be misdirected. How? For one thing, pakikisama, which underlines the cohesive strength of a Filipino informal group, tends to work for the dominant individual. For example, in an informal group, should he as a member of that group resist a supervisor for one reason or another, he can always justify his stand with his group and cause them to resist also the same person.

The hiya attitude, which epitomizes and supports the sensitivity of the Filipino individual, could also work against the supervisor as he is forced to restrict his control over the Filipino worker in order not to hurt the latter's feeling and ego lest he should resist the supervisor and result in the mentioned situation.

The bata system, of course, has also its limitations as it breeds envy among the rest of the supervisor's subordinates causing him to be segregated from them.

The pilosopo concept is a defense mechanism against the act of upgrading one's self in front of another person. When the supervisor is almost at equal footing with his subordinate in terms of seniority, in age and experience, such plays are not advisable as this may give rise to a serious conflict unless one gives in to the other.

In general, to deal with the shortcomings of the Filipino behavior, offshoot of the limitations of his value system, is a seemingly insurmountable task for the supervisor. But then, time and again, the supervisor encounters situations where his understanding of his subordinates' attitudes is tied up with a knowledge of his value concepts. One thing is evidently clear from situations like this confronting the supervisor—such task falls within his sphere of duty and responsibility.

The Filipino Hierarchy of Needs

Abraham H. Maslow states that needs exist in a hierarchical sequence and that man must meet the demands of his lower needs before those of the higher level can emerge. From these hierarchical relationships, Maslow deduced that satisfied needs are not motivators. For example, the satisfaction of a need for food is only a motivator when one is hungry. Our needs at a point in time depend on what we already have. If one need is satisfied another emerges to take its place. And these needs emerge in a predictable pattern. These needs are basic physiological or physical needs, safety and security needs, belonging or social needs, esteem needs, and self-realization needs.

46

The Filipino is unique. His hierarchy of needs is not exactly in the same order nor fits perfectly in Maslow's framework of hierarchy of needs. In the formula *Stimulus-Organism-Response*, the O variable, that is, the Filipino organism is different. His values are different and therefore his responses to stimulus will be different.

In the Filipino hierarchy of needs, the first need is *familism* or the need to belong to a family or group. The family in the Filipino mind is a defense against a potentially hostile world, an insurance against hunger and old age, an eternal source of food, clothing and shelter, an environment where a Filipino can be oneself. For the Filipino all the basic needs are met if you have a family or a group. All your safety and security needs are met, once you belong. *Walang masamang atin*, so they say in a family. In the family there is *pagpupuno sa kakulangan*, there is *pagtatakip ng kakulangan*. A Filipino is assured of acceptance within the family or his group. Thus the need of the Filipino to establish kinship is prolific. He establishes kinship by affinity, by consanguinity, and even by rituals and religious, civic, and social ceremonies. The family is the basic economic, social, political, psychological, religious, spiritual, and moral unit among Filipinos. The family gives the individual a high sense of security and belonging. The tightly-knitted kinship system defines precisely the behavioral relationships between members. In contrast, relationships with non-kinsmen are uncertain and delicate. There is economic sufficiency and security in the family. Interest of the family is primary to that of the individual composing it. There is super-ordination of family causes. To a Filipino, kinship and family are two most important organizing and legalizing elements in the corpus of other factors. A Filipino normally sees himself first as member of the family and only secondly as member of the outside group whether it's an office or company.

Sharing the benefits of increases in productivity equitably would dovetail well with the Filipino utang-na-loob. However, the benefit sharing should be equally shared rather than be based according to individual contribution. Furthermore, the worker can be expected to maintain company loyalty so long as the company objectives do not conflict with the implicit objectives of the nuclear family. Policy of promotion from within system is most welcomed by Filipino. High value is placed on a person in authority. Initiative is expected to come from the top. There is high regard for tradition, social position, and family name.

Each person is an outward extension of his family and kin

group. If a worker is caught stealing, it is said, *Ang pamilya niya'y mahihiya sa lipunan* (His family is shamed before society). The "shame" of the worker is the "shame" of the family and kin group. Even when an individual has ignored a "shaming" remark or situation, his family may take up the issue for the family position is involved. Criticism of a person is not as an individual *qua* individual, but as a representative of a family and kin group. There are cases in which incompetent schoolteachers were not fired because such an action would make both the dismissed person and his relatives *kahiya-hiya*. The supervisors themselves fear that the relatives of the dismissed person may do them actual physical harm, in addition to the inevitable threats and reprimands for the supervisors' harsh and terrible treatment. Furthermore, Filipinos do not distinguish, in general, the person from the role which he is playing. Hence, the criticism of a man's work as such is taken as a criticism of him as a person, reflecting upon his family as well. Employers and supervisors hate to fire incompetent workers. Among Philippine scholars, students, and scientists, there is almost no critical review of one another's work. The bluntness of Americans and other Europeans is not understood, but tolerated because they are "foreigners" and outside of the social system.

The second need of the Filipino in the hierarchy is the need to be *reciprocated*. This is based on the utang-na-loob value, a behavior wherein every service received, favor, or treatment accomplished has something in return. The Filipino has a high sense of personal dignity. His dignity and honor are everything to him, so that the wounding of them, whether real or imagined, becomes a challenge to his manhood. He respects other people but they must also respect him. Many a conflict between a foreign superior and a Filipino subordinate is founded on a disregard on the one hand, and a sacred regard on the other, of individual dignity. The foreigner is apt to underestimate the *dayaw* (dignity) of the Filipino. He idolizes, perhaps, the individual dignity of his foreign superior but he demands the same treatment; if not, he loses his self-control because he feels that he has been wronged or insulted though the cause itself may be trivial or slight.

According to the findings of Dr. Angelina Ramirez,[7] Filipino workers find the following reasons of vital importance in work satisfaction:

(1) He expects to be treated as an individual with dignity.

48

(2) He wants to carry on an open communication and get feedback from those he works with.

(3) In the context of performance appraisals, he wants to be rated high because the benefits of recognition and promotion go with it.

(4) He wants to be given credit for any participation which results to the productivity of the organization.

(5) He works best with co-workers who are socially supportive.

(6) He wants to be involved in challenging tasks which provide calculated risks but he is resistant to change when new behavior is required from him which he is not ready for.

The abovementioned reasons are manifestations of the need for reciprocity. Docility, the courteous, almost euphemistic speech characteristic of Filipinos searching for and giving expected answer, avoiding a negative response, and the use of go-between on an exploratory level of interactions are mechanisms for bridging the social distance between non-kinship and to serve as social devices for reducing possible friction.

Thus, productivity bargaining where fringe benefits are exchanged for improvement in output has high chances of success in the Filipino factory due to the reciprocity needs. To the Filipino employee, consistency in the superior's style of leadership would seem to have a heavier bearing than the style itself. It would be a good practice to give equitable shares of the resulting income increases in exchange for efforts of the workmen to improve the company performance. Management by objectives where employees are evaluated and directed according to a set of determined objectives would be highly successful and would be welcomed. Positive criticism is definitely acceptable to the Filipino workers as long as it is done in euphemistic and indirect way. Filipino supervisors seek interpersonal harmony with subordinates by blurring the differences and by agreement not to disagree at least openly. There is avoidance of verbal clashes. Negative criticism should be done indirectly *(Bato-bato sa langit, tamaan ay huwag magagalit)*.

Credit and collection is a problem in the Philippines because of the need to be reciprocated. An example of this is the Tagalog statement, *Siya ay may utang sa akin ngunit ako ay nahihiyang singilin siya* (He owes me a debt but I am ashamed to collect it).

Debt in the Philippines is not purely economic, but has marked social overtone. The loaning of money and goods establishes an allegiance having some similarities to "ritual kinship" in which the debtor is in subordinate position, but in which there are still reciprocal obligations. Thus, if the lender should press for the repayment of the debt he would cause the debtor hiya, for it would be implied that the debtor is unwilling to repay the debt and unaware of his obligations. The statement that "I am ashamed to collect the debt" implies a "fear" of collecting the debt, for if the debtor is "shamed" violence may occur.

Ideal interpersonal reciprocal relations among Filipinos are illustrated by the following statement: "No word is uttered, not an act is done, especially if it concerns a fellow human being, without thought of how others will be affected by it." Foreigners have frequently pointed out that equivocation, "white lies," and euphemistic discourse to avoid unpleasant truths are characteristically Filipino, making an attempt not to embarrass or to displease other persons. The Filipino anticipates and gives the expected answer, avoiding if possible a negative reply. Hence, a question by a person seeking a positive answer concerning, for example, the quantity of payment for service rendered will be invariably answered with "It's up to you."

No wonder Filipinos are most eager to fraternize in their places of work and would feel frustrated and irritated if prohibited from doing so. Because of the need to be reciprocated, it is noteworthy to observe the unwanted sort of connection between the positive and the negative traits of the Filipino. Such connection is seen in: (1) utang na loob and favoritism; (2) indiscreet hospitality and overdependency; (3) oversolicitude for *mabuting pakikisama* with somewhat dishonest equivocity or white lies; (4) tayo-tayo small group centeredness with nepotism and favoritism; and (5) between hospitality and extravagance.

Reciprocity value affects the Filipino concept of property. He considers his property as his property, public property as his property because of the *sakop* system, and his neighbor's property as his own property because of the *kapitbahay* system.

The third need in the Filipino hierarchy of needs is *social acceptance*, that is to be taken by his fellows for what he is or what they believe him to be, and be treated in accordance with his status. The Filipino needs to be socially accepted by the people who can help him in time of need. He must develop and cultivate their goodwill so as to get along with them for they are psychological investment for future economic, religious, social, and political gains. Conformity to their codes is rewarded with cooperation and assistance and non-conformity is punished by withdrawal of support. Here there is an interplay of the pakikisama value, the practice of yielding to the will of the leader or to the group as to make the group's decision unanimous.

Contest where individuals compete for recognition would be a threat to social approval and acceptance. Personality matching in work teams has both advantage and disadvantage in the Filipino cultural system. The disadvantage is in the strong possibility that social acceptance would be more difficult to achieve in a diverse group. The advantage lies in the variety and the fact that differences in roles played reduce competition since each one can contribute to the group's goals in his own unique way.

The fourth need in the Filipino hierarchy is the *social mobility* need. Once the social acceptance need is satisfied, the social mobility need arises. Social class is usually based on economic factors. Most Filipinos want to make more money to climb the social ladder. If they are given help to achieve this goal, they will do so. Those needing the most help, but with the most to gain are the low-paid workers. The Filipino, in this level, works for an upward socioeconomic mobility.

For the Filipino, evaluation by an authority or superior would be welcomed but not by subordinates or peers because of his desire for socioeconomic mobility. The Filipino employee sees his mobility as guaranteed if it were determined by his superior rather than by his peers or subordinates which can even threaten his socioeconomic climb up the ladder.

Promotion by seniority seems to be more acceptable to the Filipino than promotion by performance because mobility is not threatened if one were to have a firm hold on one's position by virtue of seniority in the company. Furthermore, the Filipino concern for authority does not go beyond the authority figures he first encounters in the company.

The fifth need in the Filipino hierarchy is *pagkabayani* ("being a hero"). This is the highest of the need levels. Here enters the values of "honor," "dignity," and "pride." Here enters the value of hiya which in Pilipino in the broadest sense is best defined as "self-esteem." This is one of the most important concepts in the social psychology of the Filipino because in it are found almost all of the aspects of the Filipino value and motivation. In this level of need what is most important is the Filipino's image as a person per se and his achievements. He expects to be respected and to be esteemed.

Philippine Management Framework

A management framework requires an understanding of the following: the individual and motivation; individual working in groups and the emergent informal organization; the basic activities and jobs of the organization; and communication.

1. *The Individual and Motivation*

The Filipino workers should be approached as individual personalities. We have to consider his cultural value and patterns like pakikisama, utang-na-loob, hiya, our kinship network, etc., in our interaction. The culture and the socioeconomic class and background of the individual, result into differences in skills acquired, factual knowledge, basic assumptions, values, tastes, aspirations, and expectations. All of these influence the motivation of the person. It is the manager's task to discover what makes his subordinates work and what makes them work harder.

The kind of supervision or management fit for the Filipino worker depends, to a significant extent, on the attitudes of these workers. These attitudes, on the other hand, are the offshoot of the value concepts which are peculiar to a particular culture and society. For the Filipino supervisor, an understanding of the Filipino values and the concomitant attitudes thereof is indispensable. It leads to certain courses of action that do avoid the adverse consequences emanating from the misdirection of the Filipino value. Kassarjian and Stringer have noted:[8]

Filipino manager has at his disposal the very forces that so often act to dissipate his best planned initiative. Filipino workers already possess the potentials for strong loyalty, group solidarity, the necessary and effective sanctions for maintaining conformity, respect towards appropriate figures and enormous fear of being shamed.

How should the Filipino supervisor or a foreign supervisor handle his Filipino subordinates? Management cases are full of examples regarding the supervisor's role toward his subordinates. One thing is evidently clear in these cases, however, and that is: that the supervisor should maintain good rapport with his subordinates and at the same time maintain his professional and functional distance from them. Take the case of a supervisor who closely supervised his subordinates to the point of shouting at and scolding them with the view that in this way they will produce what is expected of them. Instead, the workers resented him and proved to be negligent of their work. On the other hand, take the case of supervisor whose lax supervision resulted in production problems due to the workers' negligence of their work and of authority. The workers cannot be entirely blamed for their performance because their supervisors have accustomed them to do what they wanted. On the other hand, the inefficiency of the workers could be blamed on the supervisors' showing too much tolerance of their subordinates' wrongdoings. Apparently, the emphasis of the case was on the Filipino concepts of pakikisama and hiya at their extreme level. The supervisors were too closely acquainted to their subordinates that they tended to oversee the latter's undoings. Thus, though pakikisama or conformity to the codes of interaction, and hiya could yield cooperation and assistance, they also have their limitations. It is necessary for the supervisor, in handling his Filipino subordinates, to consider their attitudes and determine what action can complement these Filipino attitudes and values in order to harvest the strength of the Filipino worker.

2. *The Work Group and the Emergent Informal Organization*

The organizational chart and the work manual define the formal organization and the required behavior; but in any organization, an informal group develops internally and emerges over and above that which is formally given as required. Filipino workers tend to develop their work groups with whom they can identify and which have their own interaction patterns, sentiments, values, norms, and leaders. The Filipino supervisor can not frown on these work groups but should recognize and work with their group leaders if he wishes to manage the entire group. He should learn to deal with them so that antagonism will not develop between the formal and informal group leaders.

From the earlier discussion of the supervisor's role, tasks, needs, and responsibilities; and the attitudes that characterize the Filipino employee, it becomes necessary to touch on the atmosphere that is required to ensure a smooth interaction among Filipino supervisor and the Filipino subordinates and the work groups.

We have noted that there are two basic needs of the supervisor, namely those needs emanating from his superiors and those emanating from his subordinates. Authority and ample rights to represent management to the workers are what he requires from his superiors. The supervisor has little control over this need in the sense that it is his superiors who determine the measure or extent of his authority. On the other hand, he has some control over the needs determined by his subordinates' attitudes, that is, he can opt for a certain method of influencing and interacting with them.

Part of the supervisor's responsibility is to provide support to his work group in order to read, in an effective manner, his unit's objectives. To do this, he has to possess a perceptive mind in order to gain appreciation of the formal and informal groups' needs. He must interact with company employees at the bottom level of the organizational profile. These workers are usually less educated than he is and hence they require a direct contact and interaction which entails empathy.

Take the case of a supervisor who was a product of a bata system and had enough power and mustered arrogant authority from management that he did what he thought was right without regard for the work group's norms, feelings, and expectations. While the bata system groomed him to be the prospective officer of the company, it does not guarantee that he would become an effective officer of the company. Frank Lynch has observed that Filipino supervisors "are most successful when they have a measure of autonomous authority."[9] This autonomous authority is supported by the bata system of the Filipino value. However, this system becomes misdirected if there is immunity from wrongdoings and much emphasis is placed on the protege.

3. Understanding the Basic Activities and Jobs of the Organization

The conceptual skill of the Filipino supervisor in analyzing job requirements, skills, and challenges can result into a more effective realization of management's objectives. The job attitude of the Filipino workers has also to be considered.

Undoubtedly, the supervisor must possess technical skill and knowledge because his broad responsibilities entail a right way of doing things within his area of concern. The need for technical skills and knowledge of the work and objectives of his unit must not be underestimated if he is to achieve what is expected of him given the resources and the time frame within which to achieve his objectives.

The supervisor should recognize situations that need his ability to deal with his subordinates by considering the latter's conspicuous attitude toward his work and other people. The supervisor should learn that he cannot stand apart from the workers and just influence them by "remote control." He should first establish firmly his position in his unit and consider himself as part of the work group within that unit. He should show some pakikisama to his subordinates but not to the extent that such cooperation runs counter to the unit's objectives and to the supervisors' role. The rate of learning, degree of compliance with work procedures, intensity of work, and even the attitudes of the workers are affected by the manner and approach of the supervisor. An enthusiastic plant manager of a company included in a manpower study commented that with the same equipment and labor force, there was an increase of 50% in production (actual rate is probably less) over one year when an innovated and more humane approach to supervisors was implemented.[10]

4. Communication

Effective communication is a requirement to all effective implementations and management functions. Communication should flow all over the organization so that not only the public or customers are informed but more so the employees and officers. Gaps in the organization's communication system causes preoccupation with speculation and rumor which can lead to erroneous and destructive guessing game among employees. Among Filipino workers, *balita* is "endemic" and part of the lunch and coffee breaks. Supervisors who are non-informative and monopolizers of information make their workers go to wrong source of information which rarely serves organization objectives. It is a supervisor's major responsibility to keep his workers well informed.

The supervisor has to maintain a smooth communication link between him and his subordinates. He has to do this effectively because the results expected of him are easily quantifiable, that is, in terms of how much his unit or section produces. The greatest need that Filipino workers bring to their work is their need to understand its meaning and their role in the scheme of things. In many ways, the workers are their work and they desire their identity and status from their roles as members of an organization. For the Filipino workers, the desire for job information and for human reaction and interaction are gut level needs.

The supervisor has to be task-oriented therefore, in order to produce his expected results which are determined partly by the individual worker's contribution. However, task-orientation implies a need to communicate in a short but effective manner in order to achieve results. The four kinds of job needs that a supervisor must work on his subordinates are:[11]

(1) Job Mastery—At the entry level, it is essential for people to learn the scope of a new job so that they can be reasonably proficient;

(2) Need to know the ground rules of the organization—the desire for predictability;

(3) Feedback—They want some sort of evidence, no matter how inadequately or tentatively they are appreciated, that they are members of good standing in the organization.

Only at this third level of satisfaction on the job—if they ever do—are they able to move to the fourth need;

(4) Allegiance and loyalty to the organization—At this point, the employees are ready to give of their talents and their energy with little or no reservation.

The supervisor should be a forceful and knowledgeable leader as the Filipino worker tends to look at these qualities with awe and respect. These qualities will give the supervisor control and dominance over his unit but, again, to a limited extent, of course; if we have to view the Filipino's paternalistic attitude, then the physical age of the supervisor becomes necessary relative to his subordinates' age. This may seem to be a frivolous concept but this is how the Filipinos esteem elders and it is generally advisable that this difference be emphasized. Furthermore, the supervisor should be alert on situations where he can acquiesce to his subordinates' favors without stooping down extremely to their level. It is a token of goodwill to win the worker's confidence through the emphasis of the Filipino value of utang-na-loob. Not only does this concept breed cooperation with the supervisor, but it also supports his authority in his unit. The Hong Kong University's Centre of Asian Studies on Southeast Asian Managerial Attitudes study reveals that the Filipino managers (together with the Malaysians) showed a "favorable view of subordinates combined with an unwillingness to see information sharing as appropriate. These managers are superior but benevolent. Their subordinates are respected but the boss retains the right to simply tell what to do . . . it is very distinctly Asian. . . ."[12]

The supervisor has to be diplomatic in communicating with his subordinates. The hiya concept of the Filipinos gives rise to a sensitive personality especially in relation to his group. No Filipino worker would like to be shamed in front of his work group and thus, it is better for the supervisor to communicate with his subordinates not as one group but a composition of individual workers partly responsible to the unit's output. Take the case of a high-strung garage proprietor who shouted to a novice-mechanic: "Don't pound the battery terminals, you dummy!" The latter probably heard only the word dummy, and sure enough the next time he has a chance to pound on battery terminals, he'd do it imagining that these were his boss' knuckles.[13] To communicate accurately and get through one's commands, instructions, comments, and suggestions definitely require know-how. This is not some minor human relations mumbo-jumbo. A Filipino worker or employee does not always necessarily need *lagay* (bribe) to fulfill his job; sometimes a command or instruction given by a supervisor in a courteous, respectful way or resembling a *pakiusap* (tone of request) makes him deliver the goods and achieve results. If supervisor wants his workers to respect their job positions and work, then he should first respect the worker who occupies that job position.

Finally, the supervisor must be responsible to his subordinates' needs particularly in consideration of his actions in bringing about change. Workers tend to resist change as management tends to implement it. But then, the supervisor's sensitive position qualifies him as the best agent of change. Thus, in introducing changes, he must realistically assess the nature of the relationship between his own behavior and the response of the worker. In general, people tend to accept change as long as the social values attached to service, held by the company, are not changed.

The Need of Business Organization

The concept of Filipino values and *kaugalian* (ways) permeates practically every aspect of human activity. Business organizations have not escaped the influences of these values and ways which can only be expected as the greatest single resource available to management—the human resource or manpower. An awareness of the cultural concept, therefore, can provide management with a key to a thorough understanding of human behavior in business and industrial organizations, and a realization that Filipino values and ways can, in fact, be harnessed for the fulfillment of corporate objectives and for industrial development.

An organization is a group of people organized for some definite purpose. Since the prime factor in the attainment of the purpose of the organization is "people," it is important that an adequate and comprehensive understanding of people and human nature be seriously considered. As such, the cultural values and attitudes of people within the organization are vital elements of human behavior which have to be comprehended if the organization is to be capable of aptly coping with any situation.

The job of a supervisor or manager is to attain intended organizational objectives by working effectively with and through the human and material resources of the firm. Thus, it is of utmost importance that a balance between what people are and what people do should be struck. What people are consists basically of their cultural needs and aspirations. Thus, the importance of considering the implication of Filipino values to the management functions.

Business management can benefit from an awareness of these cultural concepts in five different ways:

1. It enables the manager to understand the behavior of people in his organization. Perceptions, attitudes, and behavior have all been, in a large measure, learned from culture.

2. The patterned life-experience of people determines to a large extent their behavior in certain situations.

3. A knowledge of culture will enable the manager to exercise control over his employees. The manager, in guiding the organization toward its goals, must also manipulate various resources at his command, including human resources.

4. It provides a substitute for experience. Awareness of the cultural factors could reduce the amount of time a person has to live in an organization assimilating its value system.

5. It aids in facilitating change. Managers must understand the nature of these values and attitudes and the needs which they serve if they wish to effect changes in their organization.

The need for management to motivate its employees has become increasingly important. Frequently, too little is done to find out what really motivates the Filipino worker to insure that appropriate motivational techniques are applied. All too often when productivity lags, or when the employee turnover is high, management hurriedly attempts to motivate employees by some means of monetary inducement, or perhaps promises of promotion. Most often, the results of these inducements are unsatisfactory.

For a long time, organizations in the Philippines have been trying to increase worker productivity by increasing pay, providing better working conditions and offering greater fringe benefits. But still the industrial output productivity is stagnant or even lags behind. Perhaps the major motivational factor of these employees is not monetary; perhaps it is related to their work environment or to the way they are treated by their superiors.

The key to unlocking increased productivity lies not so much in giving employees more, but in *managing* them better, that is, managing with a unique concern for balancing individual needs with organizational goals. Business organizations are profit-oriented and the main concern is how to keep the employees contribute to their highest level. It is usually forgotten that employees are human beings and therefore, need to be induced and motivated if they are to produce their maximum output. Management should recognize what factors motivate or become sources of dissatisfaction to their employees. Motivation relates to needs employees desire to satisfy. When action is taken to satisfy these needs, there is motivation to achieve them.

Hicks formulated a sequence which goes something like this:[14]

$$Need \quad \xrightarrow[\text{to}]{\text{leads}} \quad Motivation \quad \xrightarrow[\text{to}]{\text{leads}} \quad Actions$$

Nearly all conscious behavior is motivated or caused.

Productivity, A Matter of Values

The Center for Research and Communication in a study affirmed that in the ultimate analysis, the "best" productivity inducing technique for a business establishment depends on cultural and other factors indigenous to the country where the workers originate.[15] It further affirms that understanding men means knowing their aspirations and frustrations. It means sharing with them some of the powers over their working lives that managers habitually exercise.

Productivity is defined as the ratio of output to input. Labor productivity is the relation between total output and the amount of working hours needed to produce that total output. Net labor productivity is total output less other input factors divided by

60

labor input. Labor productivity increases when capital equipment and facilities are more efficiently used, when quality of labor itself improves, and if other favorable factors are present. Several means of increasing productivity are increased mechanization or capital investment, improving the quality of workers, better organization of work, maintaining a high level of efficiency, and increasing manpower, frugality in the procurement and use of materials, effective maintenance of equipment, and efficient inventory control system.

All the abovementioned techniques of productivity indicate the need for a strong, adequate manpower or human resources who know not only the "how to" of the job but also "want to" do the job in the best possible way. Thus, we talk of competence and motivation. Organizational theory affirms that motivation is a matter of organizing jobs according to prevalent needs as related to situation, which if properly carried out results in efficient job structure and consequent favorable job attitudes. Industrial engineering makes man a machine, economically, such that a system of incentives combined with efficient use of the human machine leads to optimal organization of work and also positive job attitudes. Behavioral science concerns itself with group and individual sentiments, and socio-psychological climate of the organization with the end of instilling healthy attitudes through human relations techniques and incentive schemes, again with the effect of drawing out positive attitudes. We are interested in this study on the behavioral approach to productivity based on Filipino values.

From the preceding explanation of the Filipino hierarchy of values, we can see that what motivates a Filipino is not just one factor, but a combination of many factors or values. Studies of labor market areas made by the Asian Labor Education Center in the University of the Philippines reveal that 90 percent of workers in the Metro Manila area, where there is a significant concentration of industrial and manufacturing establishments are recruited from the provinces.[16] This means that almost all the workers, regardless of their level of skills in our embryonic industrialization process, are socialized in a basically rural-agricultural setting. The significant change in the orientation of the formal educational system is another set of related factors that must be recognized as an important matrix for the socio-psychological considerations affecting productivity of workers in the Philippines. The educational discovery and critical thinking has produced young workers who question the purpose and operation of industry and who are reluctant to accept traditional managerial authority. Workers coming from a basically rural-agricultural setting pass through a very rough transition in adjusting to the discipline, environment, and requirements of industrial society. In contrast to the pace and tempo of work in the province, they are now to follow schedules and meet deadlines. In contrast to the informal atmosphere in the province where people regardless of their role and station in the production process call each other by their nicknames, role functions in the industrial setting are formally and clearly defined, and relationships are largely contractual. These workers are not suited for formalities such as that of applying for a leave of absence; thus absenteeism is rampant in many companies in the Philippines. A significant number of workers would simply leave or absent themselves to attend a town fiesta or a family celebration without the formality of applying for a leave of absence. Such pattern of behavior affects productivity. On the other hand, the entry of young blood with new frame of mind demands that adjustments in the area of social relations in production to harness their enthusiasm and the desire to be expressive of their capabilities must have to be evolved.

Many studies show that job dissatisfaction appears directly related to short job cycles, lack of autonomy and control over work-place, and jobs which require attention but not challenge. The psychological predisposition of workers to respond negatively to highly routinized, non-challenging work, and to exploitative social relations in work organization have given rise to such problems as absenteeism, slow turnover, low productivity, low morale, and even sabotage.

Based on the Filipino hierarchy of needs, we can say that what motivates Filipino workers to be productive are a personalistic family atmosphere in the company; attention to the emotional aspect of organization life, such as individual self-esteem, reciprocity between management and employees; respect for their human dignity; egalitarian treatment; flexibility in work assignment, schedules and deadlines; supportive role on the part of the officers; open communications and complete genuine information; a cooperative and fraternal reward and promotion system.

Analysis of Filipino values reveals that the Filipino's attachment and fidelity to family, country, God, and benefactors are all forms of the ethical value of loyalty—a variety of justice. If management is really honest and gives the worker what is due him, the Filipino value of utang-na-loob will make him render to the company fidelity, adherence, and service due to the feeling of a special bond of relationship and gratitude. The orientation of Filipino values is not a question of authoritative pressure nor of stereotyped instruction but of understanding, acceptance, and commitment. Filipino values are double-edged; they are negative or positive depending on the direction they take. They can be a help or a hindrance to productivity depending on how they are understood and practised. Take the value of utang-na-loob; this is one among many psycho-social concepts that relate to the theoretically fertile concept of *loob*. It can be *sama ng loob* (resentment), *kusang loob* (initiative), or *lakas ng loob* (courage). A Filipino, many times, is not led by principles but by circumstances, by situations and therefore, does not possess a very unique personality solely his own but rather a personality made up of where he is or what he is doing. He is situation-oriented, alert to opportunities, and indulges in a kind of situation-ethics. He has an anticipatory personality; he is ahead of reality.

Three basic values that motivate and control an immense amount of Filipino behavior are social acceptance by people of high social status who can be potential financial aid, economic security or ability to meet ordinary material needs through one's family or group, and social mobility or advancement up the social scale to another class or higher positions.

Other Considerations by the Management
1. *Pagpaplano* (Planning)

Planning is laying a course of action to achieve a desired result. It implies setting specific objectives and goals; establishing policies, programs/activities, and procedures to achieve the objectives most efficiently and effectively; and thinking through the details of the work so that the work can be accomplished with maximum certainty and economy.

In general, Filipinos are good planners.[17] They are exceptionally endowed with the ability to see through future events compared with other nationalities. In spite of this, only few Filipinos have made a breakthrough in planning. This endowment is badly offset by attitudes, values, and habits developed through periods of colonization and retained to a great extent up to the present. One such attitude is what has been popularized as the *mañana habit* or the habit of postponing work for the future.[18] The implications and effects are felt not so much during planning itself but in the implementation of the plan. It is not unusual to observe employees hurrying/cramming at the last minute because they have spent the time before the deadline leisurely.

A typical Filipino value explicitly and highly valued is the ability to get along well with others, the pakikisama or smooth interpersonal relationship.[19] As such, a Filipino manager or supervisor sees to it that the organizational plan does not in any way endanger his relationship with fellow supervisor or manager within and outside the organization whom he considers as friends. Plans may also be affected adversely because of the dominant sensitivity of the Filipino to personal affront and his desire for social acceptance.[20]

An important value that can be tapped in planning is the Filipino value of *fiesta* which makes him conceive the world as a banquet. It is a world of unlimited opportunities. But why are there many poor people? One major reason is that people forget the basics. They forget to plan. *Upang maging kahanga-hanga ang ano mang bagay na nais nating gawin, mayroon tayong batayan na masasabing mahalaga kung ito ay ating isasagawa. Unang kailangan, iplano ang ating gagawin, iplano ang bawat araw ng paggawa. Ang bawat araw ay atin upang gamitin ito. Magplano tayo. Unahin muna nating gawin ang mahahalagang bagay.*

2. *Pagtatatag* (Organizing)

Organizing is the process of identifying and grouping the tasks to be done, defining and delegating authority to carry them out and establishing the relationships which would allow people to work more effectively together in accomplishing objectives. For the latter, conditions for mutual cooperative efforts should be created and this is where small group-centeredness plays an important role.

Here we should be aware of "Filipino time." The Filipino must be educated that if he can control time, he can control the world. *Bawat oras ay mahalaga. Sa isang kompanya, ang oras ay katumbas ng pera; kaya itatag natin ang ating oras sa magandang paraan upang tayo ay hindi mahirapan sa bandang huli. Kailangang disiplinahin ang ating sarili sa pagpaplano at pagsunod sa mga ito.* Get up early and make a list! Put the most important things at the top and get going. Let the Filipino remember that there's no glory without sacrifice.

Franco gives an outline of how Pinoy organization would evolve and these are the stages:[21]

(1) The first stage is the creative or *pakulo* stage. Based on oido or hilig, he starts a business.
(2) Second stage is survival and stability which is the *jackpot* stage. He believes this as due to hard work and *bigay ng Diyos* (from God).
(3) Third stage is growth—big time, over expansion, over extension, *puede ng mag-utos* (you can command), *patseketseke* (payment by check) style of business.
(4) Fourth stage is decline or *sumasabog* stage.

3. *Paglalagay ng Tao* (Staffing)

Staffing is the function that supplies the manpower for the organization. It means more than just hiring people; hiring is just a small part of staffing. It includes defining the requirements of the job; finding the right person for the job; training, appraising, and encouraging the person to stay in his job and to accept higher responsibility when qualified.

While the Filipino is adept in defining the job and its corresponding outputs, problems come in getting the right person to do the job because of cultural values. When a Filipino manager is faced with a vacancy in his organization, first and foremost consideration is fitting in the persons he knows, the person with whom he feels he has a quasi-obligation to do some favor. First in the test would be jobless relatives who or whose parents helped him one way or another in the past. This is commonly termed utang-na-loob.[22] While it facilitates the recruitment process, it also has some setbacks on the quality of the output the person has to deliver. If we examine the recruitment process, majority comes in because of what is known as "the proper connection." When one has landed a job the common questions asked are inquiries about the *padrino* or the proper connection. Another Filipino value related to staffing is *lakad* system. Lakad is derived from the Tagalog term, meaning "to walk"—but, in Filipino social psychology, it means "to fix things for someone." If one wants to be employed in some firms where there are Filipinos, the approach is to look for an insider to facilitate the processing. Related to this is the *bata* system. Old employees who are proteges of a boss are considered "almighty" by the new employees. *Makikibagay ka riyan—bata iyan ng boss* (You'd better learn to deal with him—

he is the protege of the boss).

In assigning responsibilities within an organization, relationships whether consanguineous or otherwise is first consideration for the Filipino. The person's ability is a secondary factor. For the Filipino, the popular dictum is *walang masamang atin.*

4. *Pamamahala* (Directing)

Directing means more than just telling people what to do. Since management at all levels deals with several people, directing in a broad sense means running the team. It means more than giving directions in the sense of giving orders. It means determining the directions in which the team should go, that is, guiding, instructing, counselling, motivating, leading subordinates to achieve goals. Effective directing requires leadership and motivation.

The Filipino generally has a high regard for authority or what we call "authority hang-up" such as "a plus in his staff development" or "he has potentials which could be realized with this job and will be useful to the organization." To direct properly there is a need for mental make-up or *kaayusan ng pag-iisip.* One must accept himself as he is—*Harapin mo ang katotohanan at huwag matakot* (Face the truth and do not fear). *Pagkatapos magpasiya ka kung ano ang dapat mong gawin* (decide what you want to do); *magpasiya ka kung ano ang isusuko mo* (decide what you will have to give up); *magpasiya ka kung papaano mo ito uumpisahan* (decide how to begin); *huwag kang matakot magpasiya* (decide and live with the decision). *Ipakita mo ang iyong tunay na pagkatao; ipakita mong ikaw ay may kakayahan sa buhay at iwasan mong maging "plastic."*

With the development of organizational systems, the occurrence of similar flaws in staffing has been reduced but not totally wiped out. It is because this value is supported highly by the Filipino society in general. These acts are not directly done for purely individual success but for the economic and social betterment of one's *kababayan*, relative, or friend.[23] With some modifications on the objectivity of the Filipino, the purpose and objectives of the staffing function could be attained very satisfactorily in getting things done by the subordinate.[24] But again, this is complicated by corollary values such as pakikisama, utang-na-loob, and fatalism.

When faced with hardship in work or in life in general, the usual recourse is *bahala na ang Diyos* (it is up to God). To some extent, when the supervisor displays excellent capabilities and charisma in the job, hero worship or "treatment next to God" is often exhibited by the supervisor. This could be frustrating to the subordinates if they forget the fact that the god supervisor is also human and can commit mistakes.

In directing, the motivation of the person must also be considered. To some extent, Abraham Maslow's hierarchy of needs would not apply to Filipinos in general. For Filipinos, the need for respect and dignity is as basic as the physiological and security needs. Thus, the importance of *pakikipag-usap* or communication. *Ang pakikipag-usap ay isang paraan ng pagdaloy ng impormasyon o kaalaman at pagkakaunawaan ng bawa't tao.*

5. *Pagkokontrol* (Controlling)

Controlling means measuring and evaluating the progress of the work done with the plan. It also includes taking steps to see to it that deviations from plans are checked and corrected.

Assessing the performance of subordinates is a sensitive aspect of the supervisor's job. Among Filipinos, the tendency of distorting the results of this function is great primarily because of cultural values. When frankness is demanded in the evaluation of performance, the Filipino supervisor is put in an extremely hard position of finding ways to indirectly inform the person concerned. Offense must be avoided even in the realm of facing job realities. Pakikisama is also considered if only to pressure the interpersonal order in the organization.[25]

A behavior pattern which can be used in controlling is the popular conversational technique called *sociostat*. This can regulate social behavior. Words or remarks such as *TY* (Thank you), *Mahiya ka naman!, Ano 'ng say mo?, Makisama ka naman, Nakakahiya iyan, Pare, tama na 'yan* can control the Filipino subordinate's behavior. *Kantiyawan* and Bato-bato sa Langit approach would be another method. Praise the Filipino in public but criticize or reprimand him in private.

Filipino Values and Their Implication to the Management Functions

Most Filipino values arise and obtain their strength around the *system of kinship;* consequently these values generate employee practices or behavior different from those prescribed by the formal organization. *Familism* is a major determinant for the existence and influence of Filipino values in the theoretically different orientation of a formal organization. Familism is best understood in terms of intergenerational reciprocal assistance among the members. The member of any given nuclear Filipino family is in reality never alone. There always exists a psychological bond among family members so that even if they are geographically separated from each other, they know that they can always activate such bond whenever a need for assistance arises. Difficulties are thus oftentimes softened by the knowledge that there are relatives who are always there and willing to help in times of need.

It is this value orientation that provides some sense of psychological security to the Filipino and which enables him to surmount the varying demands of his environment. Familism has provided the Filipino with a protective shield which makes him less vulnerable to the various crises in life. To the Filipino, kinship is a protection shell. When he thinks of kinship, he is thinking of comfort and security. The idea of *kamag-anak* (relative) is perhaps one of the most central symbolisms in his mind. It is a moral symbol. The very idea of it automatically invokes some kind of commitment to others. In brief, the fundamental basis on which Filipino social behavior unfolds is found in one's kinship relations. Relationship with one's kin is a precondition to general social participation so that when one is unable to effectively participate in social life he is often perceived as *walang kamag-anak*. Hence, the Filipino's sense of inner security is not based on a tough-minded sense of individuality but on a consciousness that he has relatives and that they are always ready to aid him.

He is therefore easily threatened by the unfamiliar and the unknown. When he goes to another place, he tries to find out whether he has any relatives in that area. If not, at least a friend is important to him. If one is not available he draws himself close to someone with whom he can establish a relationship that is close to 'kinship'.

The complex and impersonal structure of a formal organization threatens the inner security of the individual worker. Because of his historical experience, he does not respond to the situation by being more competent in his work. His first consideration is to establish a kin-like relationship with his superiors and friends. When his boss becomes a *compadre* (godfather), the work situation becomes less threatening because he knows for sure that he has a relation who will assist him in his needs. The Filipino becomes a child under his boss' protective wings. He becomes secure in knowing that there is someone who will always fight for him, who will help him during times of stress, and will go beyond limits.

Everything a Filipino does is personalized in terms of kin-like relationships. These relationships cut across various dimensions of the Filipino's social sphere. One is not only an employee but at the same time a friend, a relative, a brother, a compadre, etc. The same perception is accorded the superior. In view of this, it is not uncommon that we find in a formal organization a strong sense of personal loyalty not to the organization but to the superiors. The commitment is not to the goals of the organization but to the incumbent officers. Clearly, the employee's response is to view the existing formal organization as the oppressor. He does not comprehend the impersonal nature of the organizational system because in his social life the dominant value-orientation is personalism. In short, the formal requirements of an organization deviate from his system of value-orientation; in fact, it is only here where a different set of values is demanded of him. While deviant, it is not at all influential in his day-to-day social participation. Hence, instead of changing his broad social network to fit this deviant one, what generally happens is that he "readjusts" the norms of the formal organization to fit his entire spectrum of social perspective. Thus, the values and attitudes of lagay, lakad, utang-na-loob, pakikisama, bata-bata, etc. pervade the formal system because these are essential aspects of the Filipino dominant value-orientation.

It is clear that various organizational structures both professional and private, which are supposed to operate in an objective and impersonal manner, never operate in this way because the variant value-orientation is being subverted in favor of the dominant personalistic value-orientation.

The Filipino's value-orientation toward personalism or personal loyalty to the people he has labeled as 'kins' enables his values to exert an influence over his behavior and actions. The presence of *role conflict* within an employee is largely responsible why his values create behavior or practices that are deemed deviant, subverting those of the formal organization's.

The Filipino defines his role or patterns of behavior which he deems appropriate to his particular position in society. This definition of role reflects his values which, in turn, are derived from his reference groups, that is, groups to which he actually belongs or which acceptance he seeks. These values define his role requirements. Since the Filipino has various reference groups and occupies various positions, he has many roles to play. For example, a Filipino officer in an automotive manufacturing company may also be the head of a family or a relative to persons 'A,' 'B,' and 'C' and must act out the roles of an employee, a family man, and a relative.

The roles may conflict, in which case, the Filipino officer finds himself occupying position with incompatible role requirements.

When such conflict arises, which of the roles will he then carry out? When the carrying out of role one is rewarded or not punished (or if the performance of the alternative role is less rewarded but more punished), it is more likely that the Filipino officer will carry out role one. Another important consideration is the person's choice of reference groups from among various groups: the greater the ability of the group to confer prestige upon the individual, the more likely he will employ it as a frame of reference. The personality characteristics of the individual, his rate of social mobility, and his location in the membership groups are the other factors which determine the choice of the reference group.

When an individual enters a business firm, he places himself in an organization and must operate within a formal structure; a system of rules and objectives defining the tasks, processes, and procedures of participants according to some officially approved pattern. The business firm may become a reference group. However, in joining a company, the employee brings along his values which are supported by other groups such as his family, class or peer group. These values make the individual play other roles in addition to that of an employee.

Role Conflicts

Role conflicts occur when the employee must act out the expectations of reference groups with contradictory values. Using Parson's pattern variables, for example, the business firm requires of its employees a collectivity orientation rather than self-orientation, universalism rather than particularism. On the other hand, primary reference groups such as his family and clan require self-orientation rather than collectivity orientation, particularism rather than universalism. In this situation, the employee resorts to certain practices for which he is rewarded or for which he is not punished.

Take for example an employee who reports to work on time and observes office hours. He is requested by his officemates to be like the rest of them who report late and who go out shopping during office hours. "*Makisama ka naman,*" (Go along with us), he is told. This employee finds that this is contrary to his sense of duty but he may soon give in to his colleagues if only to avoid being ostracized.

Take these other instances: Employee 'A' does not 'pad' his travelling expenses and prepare his travelling expenses voucher accordingly. His colleagues ask him to accomplish a travelling expenses voucher like theirs which has been altered. "*Para hindi naman kami mapahiya,*" (So we won't be shamed), they say. This contradicts A's sense of honesty. However 'A' may soon give in if only to please the others.

Employee 'B' thinks it is not proper to bring home bond paper, pencils, or erasers for personal use and does not do so. However, he sees his officemates doing it and realizes that what he considers improper may save a lot of trouble and so he follows suit. Besides, by not availing of such an opportunity he thinks he has lost an advantage *(nalamangan)*.

Employee 'C' uses the firm's car in bringing his children to school since everybody else does it. This saves him a lot of trouble and besides it is status-conferring.

Employee 'D' may once have been the recipient of a large favor from a friend. In return, employee 'D' uses his authority to find a position for his friend in his company, even if it is obvious to him that his friend is not competent for the job.

Employee 'E' brings in goods to the office during working time and office work is relegated to the background, as arguments over the quality and prices of items follow. Peddlers who come around almost always succeed in getting the employees away from their desks. During all this time, the other people in need of these employees' services try vainly to attract their attention, for if they are not out shopping, employees are doing something else such as chatting or reading newspapers.

At eight o'clock in the morning, employee 'F' is not yet in or at four-thirty, he has already stopped working or gone home.

Sometimes, employee 'G' absents himself but such absences

71

are not charged against his leave credits.

Employee 'H' uses the company car for his wife's marketing.

Supervisor 'I' requests his workers to repair his kitchen or his roof during workdays.

The salaries of cooks and gardeners of manager 'J' are paid out of company funds in the banks or other business offices of manager 'J'.

Representation allowances are availed of by manager 'K' even if not needed in his job.

Warehouse manager 'L' sells raw materials to middlemen who, in turn, sell these to other users. In other cases, employees are asked to pay for company-provided items.

Employee 'M' asks the waiter to change the receipt so that the money reimbursed would be more than what he actually spent.

These illustrations may be viewed as manifestations of lack of devotion to work and lack of commitment to one's career, which, in turn, seem to imply an absence of control on the individual's behavior. However, closer inspection of their sources would indicate the influence of an inherent value system different from that demanded by the organization and therefore the existence of role conflicts. Expressions of such behavior are therefore modes of resolving these role conflicts.

The Need for Redirection

The Filipino individual in the organization does not have only one role to play but several. These roles are played in response to the expectations of various groups and these expectations may differ depending upon the groups' value system.

Roles come into conflict because of the diversity of value sources or reference groups. The conflict between professional and private roles, between the individual role as a father or a relative, or as a member of an organization, is resolved through practices described earlier as manifestations of lack of self-discipline. These practices constitute acting out of the expectations built into his private role. The professional role into which are built contrary expectations is then carried out. The primacy of the private role persists because this mode of behavior is reinforced by the individual's other reference groups and/or because the business firm has no sanction against this mode of behavior.

On the whole, we can conclude that most Filipino values and attitudes, if not properly directed, work against organizational objectives; that is, more often than not, the values and attitudes endanger the efficient attainment of organizational objectives. Take the value of social acceptance. If misdirected, it hinders the free expression of ideas, feelings, and desires especially in cases where it entails isolation from the group. Thus, comes the preoccupation with 'face' and with appearance, with *palabas* or *pabongga* and with 'good PR'. Some Filipino values and attitudes, misdirected as they are now, have caused the breakdown of bureaucratic and organization controls, resulting in widespread nepotism and unfairness in both public and private offices. The Filipino values and attitudes of mañana habit, ningas cogon, and bahala na are certainly counter-productive.

The Filipino must respond to the challenge of the formal business organization. He must redirect his value system to acquire a new behavior in harmony with organizational goals. Management must take the necessary administrative processes in answer to the expectations and value systems of the Filipino individuals in the organization. It is of utmost importance to complement the crying needs of individuals with the task of administrative process.

Crying Needs of Individuals	*Administrative Task*
(1) *Information.* The individual in organizations needs information and understanding of the company's goals, policies and procedures, rules, and regulations. He is, most often than not, unaware of their gravity, hence his actions are uncaring and seemingly unresponsible.	(1) *Communicate.* Management should inform him about the organizational goals, policies and procedures, rules and regulations, impressing on him their importance and the management's urgent need for cooperation. An individual will exercise self-direction and self-control if motivated towards certain goals.
(2) *Opportunity.* The individual in an organization is tacitly asking for an opportunity to apply his	(2) *Challenge.* Management should challenge the individual rallying to the organizational objectives.

73

ingenuity and solidarity in the service of the company. Imagination, ingenuity, and creativity in the solution of organizational problems are needed by the individual.

Management should look upon the individual as imaginative and a potential force for the company's well-being. It should challenge, rather than push, the individual to achieve the company objectives and to observe its rules and regulations, policies and procedures.

(3) *Help, if Deficient.* Most often than not, the individual in an organization is deficient either in the proper knowledge, attitude, skills, or habits related to the job. Thus, he needs help in these areas.

(3) *Care.* Management should ascertain the individual's training needs and elicit his views. It must have plans for training him to be fully functional in his job.

(4) *Measures/Criteria/Standard of Performance.* The individual needs to be shown the objective criteria or standard of performance required of him. He must be informed that solely on the basis of these criteria will he be evaluated.

(4) *Control.* Management should devise a control system with adequate performance standard. It must objectively and uniformly implement and apply this standard of performance to all the individuals in the organization.

(5) *Rewards.* The individual expects a proper reward or renumeration for the task he has perfectly done. If this expectation of reward for a good work done is frustrated, he is capable of doing anything.

(5) *Compensate.* Commitment is a function of rewards associated with achievement. Management should think of a system of rewarding objectively good work and performance.

The administrative processes must be in consonance with the organizational behavior and the individual behavior in the organization. The reason is that organization is primarily concerned with the *most efficient relationships between people and functions.* The relationships of people within the organization, the feelings people have about the structure they are placed to work in, and the input of these feelings on their work are of utmost importance. Take the case of an unpleasant encounter that cannot be helped, say, if an employer or a supervisor has to reprimand a subordinate. One of the indications that an attempt is being made to lessen the hurt or minimize the unpleasantness is in his showing of concern for the person's private life. Thus, after an employer has told his employee to, say, work harder because office or plant efficiency suffers because of him, he abruptly switches to an "And how are your wife and children?" routine. This relieves the employee and makes him feel that he still belongs, is loved, and accepted. Otherwise, he resents the criticism and does not accept it. The person criticized concludes that the employer is unmindful of other people's feelings and is difficult to get doing with, *mahirap pakisamahan.* Questions such as "Are you married?" "How much do you make a month?" etc. on the part of the employer or superior to an employee or subordinate are meant to show one's concern for the other person. It is part of pakikisama.

The Filipino manager cannot run his office as impersonally as a foreigner. In many offices, one usually gets the impression that when he gets his papers processed, for instance, a personal favor has been done for him. It is not unusual, therefore, for Filipinos who have received such "favors" to feel that they should offer the company official a "reward." These rewards take the form of, say, a *kaing* (basketful) of mangoes, a box of chocolates, etc. and they are given at a "decent" time, that is, not too soon after the favor has been received. At a superficial glance, this gift-giving would seem like a form of bribery. However, the superior or officer is at a predicament. The Filipino subordinate feels "shamed" *(napapahiya)* if his token of gratitude is not received. It makes him feel that his gift is not good enough. Or he interprets it as a sign that the other party wants to end their relationship. No Filipino would probably dare ask for another favor if his token of appreciation is not accepted. It would mean that he would forever be in the other person's debt—*nakalubog na sa utang* (buried in debt). Or it can be interpreted that the person who continues to ask for favors can't take the cue that the other party doesn't want to grant him future favors. Such person is *walang pakiramdam* (literally "no feeling" i.e., callous) or *makapal ang mukha* ("thick-faced" i.e., shameless).

But debts of gratitude, big or small, cannot really be paid at all, as shown in another Filipino saying: *Ang utang-na-loob, magpakaliit man, utang at utang din kahit mabayaran. Sa pakitang loob at tapat na damay ay walang salaping sukat maitimbang.* (A favor no matter how small, is a debt we must never forget since no money can ever fully repay it.) Here is a wealth for potential foundation of the Filipino's loyalty to the company.

Generally it is desirable to get along well, to be accepted, to belong. It would be nice to be approved of too, but the Filipino often settles for acceptance. As long as he does not suffer open disapproval or rejection, it's all right with him. Thus, a Filipino employer or supervisor isn't expected to praise his employees. If he doesn't complain, that means everything is fine. If the office is running smoothly, then the Filipino employer or supervisor is happily quiet about it. It is when things go wrong that he makes himself heard. This is probably one reason why most Filipino employers and supervisors seem to emphasize the negative, to play up what is wrong in the company and to be quiet about what is right.

In spite of the *Filipino time* attitude, experienced managers and superiors make time budgeting a prerequisite to any significant action. Deadlines, in Philippine setting, may not be necessarily inducements to speedy action, since there is usually the expectation in the Filipino's mind that there will be an extension anyway. However, deadlines must still be emphasized as checkpoints and to keep interested personnel aware of what should be accomplished and alert to any subtle loss of momentum. In spite of Filipino time mentality, a judgment should be made on the time required for any project. Experience may tell that longer time should be provided to be realistic but projection and assessment of time provide measurement gauges. Time awareness and measurement should be emphasized among Filipinos in organizations, considering the bahala na cultural syndrome.

Filipino managers or supervisors who are time and deadline conscious are sometimes branded by their subordinates as articulate, that is *maarte na, makulit pa.* For instance, when the manager or supervisor presses on the submission of a progress report on the due date, the Filipino subordinate's response is typically complete frustration. *"Ang kulit nito,"* which freely translated could be "much ado about nothing." In other words, to this subordinate the progress report or the things to be accomplished and thus be reported are irrelevant, too fast, too remote, too unimportant. Thus, the importance of continuous follow-up and value clarification to the Filipino subordinate.

With regard to effective utilization of manpower resources, a business organization must have a standard of selection toward which Filipino values can be directed to attain compatibility between position/job assignment and employee's talent. To assign people to particular positions because of hiya, awa, bata system, nepotism, favoritism, utang-na-loob without following objective and appropriate standards makes the organization vulnerable to any downfall trend. No wonder some companies have departments composed of 50 people who turn out less work than their competitors in a similar department which is staffed by one-half the number.

Leadership by Filipino Values

Leadership can be described as a process of influence on a group in a particular situation, at a given point in time, and in a specific set of circumstances that stimulate people to strive willingly to attain organizational objectives, giving them the experience to attain the common objectives and satisfaction with the type of leadership provided.

Leadership must be based on the insight into present realities. Leaders who succeed are those who can get inside their people and motivate them. A leader gets inside people so as to energize them. Leadership on the job can be viewed as the ability to influence the thinking, attitude, and activities of others so that they willingly direct their behavior toward organizational objectives. For these purposes, four sets of variables are important: (1) personality of the manager; (2) personality of the group; (3) situation in which leadership is exercised; and (4) organizational factors.

A leader must understand the group. A group consists of two or more people who have an explicit psychological relationship to each other. A leader must accommodate his leadership actions to the mandates of the situation. He must know the organizational realities and givens that have taken root to which he must become attuned. Every company has its own unique history, tradition, values, folkways, mores, taboos, and unwritten rules of conduct; each has its peculiar power structure and its own ways of cooperating, coordinating, and getting the job done.

In the Philippines, group activities are organized in terms of kinship and common economic and ritual interests. One or more families form the core of this group activities, the leadership usually being provided by the dominant family or families. Wealth and the size of a man's family and kinship group are the primary determinants of leadership.

In recognizing a leader, more often than not, a Filipino sees the superficial realities rather than the internal qualifications for leadership. Observe the status syndrome in urban business communities and organizations. Business leadership is identified with people who are wearing coat and tie, credit-card, and have white-collar job. In other situations, people elected to be leaders are Filipinos who do not contradict, displease, show anger, or otherwise exercise their critical faculties. This is because the Filipino society is a peasant society which reflects the long history of its people as peasants. Ideally, people in a peasant society should get along well and not show anger. When community residents depend greatly on one another's good will and assistance in order to keep the normal round of community activities operating, then pleasantness becomes mandatory. Criticism makes enemies and leads to feuds and reprisals.

On the other hand, in city life and industrialized sectors, leadership is often identified with the fiery speakers and *bomba*-type politicians and demagogues, whose aggressiveness and *bravura* (courage) will make others and management tremble as we can see in unions, gangs, and student organizations. These urban groups would prefer a leader who is *lumalaban* (that fights), dares to offend, expresses criticism and disagreement.

In general, Filipinos identify leadership with benevolence because of the value of *personalism*. The focus is not so much on what a person does as on who he is; not so much on what a person knows as whom he knows and who knows him; not so much on the objective reality of things as on the way things are actually perceived. A leader must temper law by "consideration" and justice by "feeling." He must not press the "hot button" unless a man's subjective core of self-worth is somehow touched. A leader must be always careful not to offend and, of course, not to be offended. His appeals to his subordinates must be shown or presented *subjectively*, not distantly and must be preceded by personal contact. A leader must be aware of the *bargaining* system of the Filipino before closing a commitment to attain a certain objective. He must also develop a sort of a group of followers because of the Filipino value of *suki* system.

Filipinos put high value on persons in authority. Initiative is expected to come from above because the leader is considered as the expert. Thus, Filipino leaders have the tendency to cling to some powers outside himself as tradition, social position, family name, acknowledged authority to reassure himself of his worth and rightness of his acts. Sometime pabonggahan or palabas needs to be utilized by the leader to assert his authority. In fact, use of loud amplified speech rather than reasoned arguments is more forceful in being elected by the people as a leader.

Small-group centeredness is another Filipino value much to be considered in leadership. The Filipino finds big identity with small groups. The Filipino follower's behavior is *purposeful*, from a purely subjective viewpoint. This behavior is subjectively orderly behavior depending on his image of himself, what kind of person he is, and what he wants others to think he is. "Status symbolism" of a person and the group he joins affects his selection of the leader to follow. The group is a symbol of the status of the person varying according to how much it is associated with individual needs and social interaction. The Filipino is the most defensive follower. Some Filipinos will follow a leader because they like him.

In a scientific study made on the intracultural comparison of the Filipino concept of the ideal manager,[26] the Filipino potential managers and career managers surveyed agree that the values and characteristics of an ideal manager are the following:

(1) decision-making
(2) future planning
(3) developing new methods
(4) search for quantifiable variables
(5) family obligation
(6) personal friendship

They disagreed in ranking on the other hand, on the following values and characteristics of an ideal manager:

(1) maintaining status difference
(2) respect for authority

(3) risk-taking
(4) capacity to be loyal
(5) support of government
(6) religious-ethical values
(7) capacity for hard work
(8) sensitivity to other's feelings
(9) belief in subordinates

How to Build Leadership

There are two kinds of leader. One is the kind who uses authority and compels grudging obedience by his followers. The other kind inspires, persuades, and sets an example. The latter is the more acceptable type in the Philippine setting.

A leader must possess a certain degree of imagination and vision. He must be able to think ahead—to visualize and plan on beyond the immediate present. He must also have a goal; his goal must be practical and right. For this, he must have the foresight to realistically create plans and programs leading to that goal. A leader in the Philippines must first of all have a clear concept of what is possible in the Philippine realities and a clear concept of what his Filipino followers want. He must be alert, ahead of those who are following him to chart the course ahead and be able to decide the right course of action when problems come up. A leader must know how to work with other people. He must command the admiration and respect of the Filipino followers in order to get their trust, loyalty, and responsiveness. Furthermore, he must be able to organize them that they achieve their maximum potential under his guidance. Genuine friendliness and outgoing concern for others are two qualities Filipino subordinates look for in a leader. They need a leader who has time for a smile; a friendly chat; and shows sincere interest in their lives, hopes, and dreams. He builds a sense of comradeship with them without losing their respect for him. A leader always communicates. He has trained himself to think clearly, and therefore he is able to express himself with clarity and persuasiveness to his subordinates. He is able to create a unity of purpose among his subordinates and achieve vigorous action out of otherwise dissimilar group. He accepts the responsibility for the mistakes of the subordinates he himself has selected and give his subordinates public credit for their triumph. He willingly delegates authority to others and organizes those functioning under him to accomplish the objectives.

A true leader must consistently set an example of fairness, integrity, and high moral character. Self-discipline is an absolute must for a Filipino if he is a man of leadership. A true leader is not afraid of problems. *Hindi takot humarap sa problema.* He thinks positively. He has clear and orderly line of thinking *(maayos at tiyak na pag-iisip).* He has *kakayahang magtatag ng pagpupulong at mabisang pamamahala sa mga tao.* He has *kakayahang himukin ang mga tao sa pagtatamo ng mga layunin.* He has *kakayahang humarap sa iba't ibang kalagayan.* He has *mga mungkahi para sa pagpapaunlad.*

The First Lady, Mrs. Imelda Marcos, has a very relevant definition of leadership:[27]

Leadership is putting things in the center. It's good to know your *right.* It's good to know your *left.* But you cannot stay on your right forever—you will flip over. You cannot stay on your left, either. You have to anchor yourself where you are strongest. Here in the center and the center is yourself: Filipino. Our strength is our ownselves. Our being Filipino. A lot of the power of leader in the Philippine setting is his sensitivity to be able to know what the people need. Sensitivity to one's fellow human being will make a leader do everything he can to meet his needs.

In the Philippine industries, a good managerial leader will see to it that adequate training will be provided for the workers. He will be concerned with their health. He will provide recreational facilities and opportunities for them. He will structure work assignments so that the worker will find them at least interesting—and, if possible, challenging. He will compensate the workers fairly and make certain that the fairness of the compensation is not merely a unilateral judgment of the management. He knows that unless a worker feels that he is fairly compensated, he is not likely to put forth his best efforts. He does all effort to provide the worker with an adequate sense of security.

A leader creates an atmosphere of approval of workers. He makes clear to them that he genuinely approves of them even though he may sometimes criticize them. He makes certain the worker knows what is expected of him. He gives the worker a clear picture of company policy, the requirements of his job, and role of his superior. He gives the worker advance knowledge of changes that will directly affect him. He knows his workers as individuals.

He is familiar with each worker's interests, capabilities, and ambitions. He gives them his unqualified support as long as their actions are consistent with what they are supposed to do. He develops activities and symbols that encourage loyalty to the organization.

The Making of a Filipino Business Leader

Most of industrial leaders' problems revolve around difference in people's values. People have a value system which includes his way of thinking about individuals, ideas and things; his beliefs and convictions; his concept of usefulness, excellence, etc. People have different backgrounds, cultures, orientations, points of view about life, different attitudes which are products of his past experiences including his education. His background has much to do with his readiness for advancement and the leadership role he assumes.

A business leader is concerned with efficiency, productivity, effectiveness, and profitability. We, Filipinos, are told that the models of efficiency are the German or the Swiss. But efficiency is only in relation to a purpose or an objective. A leader that strives for efficiency must spell out individual or corporate objectives and has a systematic or orderly approach to attaining an objective; he has a well-planned, step-by-step method of arriving at the desired result. Nothing is left to change or improvisation syndrome. Filipino workers and sometimes even managers and executives love to improvise. There is implanted in them that sort of mental laziness, the oido (by hearing). Thinking ahead is simply nonsense to many Filipinos. A leader must distinguish between doing things *according to the rules* and doing the *right things to do*. Nevertheless, the Filipino leader must have efficiency consciousness and capacity for systematic innovation. This implies the ability to utilize effectively the analytical approach in the solution of business problems. He must have the ability to view from all points a problem which has been defined and to analyze the best solution for it.

A Filipino business leader must be a socially responsible person. He must be concerned not only about company profitability but also about social profitability. He must be able to run businesses that operate across national boundaries. He must be able to operate in diverse cultures.

82

Training in Filipino Value: A Must

In the light of the foregoing analysis, the redirection of Filipino values can only be achieved by proper training and development to improve the Filipino character and strengthen it to positive direction. There should be an inculcation of the Filipino positive traits and those that are remedial to the traditional negative directions of Filipino values. Examples of positive traits are loyalty, hardworkingness, docility, integrity, and sense of dignity. Use of direct and indirect approaches of moral formation and instruction in instilling the worthy traits should be emphasized. Prudence as a virtue in the practice of Filipino values such as pakikisama, awa, utang-na-loob should be highlighted. Constant lookout for situations where positive Filipino values may be inculcated must be management's preoccupation. The strongest form of training and development is the use of positive approach through encouragement and example by the employer, the company management and its authorities and officers.

Management must consider which of the Filipino values are important and necessary to business and industrial productivity. It must determine which of these values can they capitalize on and how they could develop management strategies adapted to the values of Filipino workers towards increased productivity. Management must study how to redirect the Filipino values in order to bring out the best in their Filipino employees.

❦

REFERENCE NOTES

[1]Keith Davis, *Human Behavior at Work and Organizational Behavior* (New York: McGraw Hill Book Company, 1972), p. 122.

[2]Peter F. Drucher, *The Practice of Management* (London: Pan Book Limited, 1973), p. 382.

[3]Ibid., pp. 386-388.

[4]Frank Lynch, "The Man in the Middle," *Philippine Journal of Public Administration*, Vol. 11, No. 3, July 1967.

[5]Ernesto A. Franco, "Management, Pinoy Style," *HR Magazine* (May 1979), p. 22.

[6]Ibid., p. 22.

[7]From a speech delivered by Dr. Angelina Ramirez.

[8]J.B.M. Kassarjian and Robert A. Stringer, Jr., *The Management of Men* (Manila: Molim's Copier Center, 1970), p.

[9]Lynch, "The Man in the Middle," p. 420.

[10]Bernardo M. Villegas and Carlos A. Abola, "Toward a More Productive Filipino Worker." (Progress Report in a research project, Center for Research and Communication, Manila, 1974.)

[11]Mary Goolsby, "The Management of Human Resource in Organization." (Paper read in celebration of the National Budget Week at Philippine International Convention Center, April 25, 1978.)

[12]Ibid., p. 9.

[13]Villegas and Abola, "More Productive Filipino Worker," p. 13.

[14]Herbert Hicks and Guillet C. Ray, *Modern Business Management: A Systems and Environmental Approach* (New York: McGraw Hill, Inc., 1974).

[15]Bernardo Villegas and Antonio N. Torralba, "Studies on Motivation and Productivity" (1974), p. 17.

[16]Manuel M. Dia, "Socio-Psychological Factors Affecting Productivity of Skilled Workers" (1980), p. 3.

[17]Julian Lopez, "The Filipino as a Planner." (A Research Paper on Management, University of the Philippines, 1968.)

[18]Adoracion Arjona, "The Ningas Cogon and the Mañana Habit," *Unitas*, Vol. 37, 1915), p. 548.

[19]Frank Lynch, *Social Acceptance Reconsidered*, IPC Paper No. 2 (Quezon City: Ateneo de Manila Press, 1970), p. 21.

[20]Frank Lynch, *Understanding the Philippines and America: A Study of Cultural Themes* (Quezon City: Ateneo de Manila Press, 1968).

[21]Franco, "Management, Pinoy Style," p. 24.

[22]Mary Hollnsteiner, "Reciprocity or a Filipino Value," *Society, Culture and the Filipino*, Vol. 1 (Quezon City: Ateneo de Manila, Institute of Philippine Culture, 1975), p. 90.

[23]F. L. Jocano and P. Mendez, "The Filipino Family in its Rural and Urban Orientation: Two Core Studies" (Manila: Research and Development Center, Centro Escolar University, 1974), p. 35.

[24]Frank Lynch, "Values and Norms," *Society, Culture and the Filipino*, p. 18.

[25]Mary Hollnsteiner, "Social Structure and Organization," *Society, Culture and the Filipino*, p. 95.

[26]Nestor N. Navarro, "A Study of the Intracultural Comparison of the Filipino Concept of the Ideal Manager" (1972), p. 46.

[27]Cynthia U. Santiago, "The First Lady Style, Management by Feeling," *HR Magazine* (September, 1979), p. 12.

Filipino Value System and Change

It is commonly said that the only permanent thing in the world is change. In fact, change is around man—in the seasons, in his social environment, and in his own biological processes. Change is a common phenomenon. It is so common and universal that the ancient Greek philosopher, Heraclitus, affirmed that we cannot take a bath in the same river twice. The continuous flow of water means that the river we see today will not be the same river tomorrow.

As a concept, change has deep historical roots. Ancient Chinese sages perceived change and developed the concept of *yin* and *yang* which they defined as the forces producing change. They recognized that change takes place always. They developed a philosophical attitude about change and its role on the life of men, governments, and states.

Change is a brute and irrational force. Inanimate matters change. Water, mountains, and hills change. Brute animals change. And even man changes. But man's change is different from the change that occurs in inanimate things and irrational beings. Man must change rationally. Furthermore, he is destined to direct change in other beings. What is important is how man is changing and in what direction. Change must have direction, for changes that lack direction can result not only in chaos but also in man's own annihilation.

Alvin Toffler in his Theory of Adaptation aims to help man cope more effectively with personal and social changes by deepening his understanding of how men respond to it.[1] According to Toffler, the three powerful forces of modern change are *acceleration*, *novelty*, and *diversity*. These forces are due to the advent of science and technology, which are: *explosion* or the increase of population; *inplosion* or the urban squeeze; *dysplosion* or the fragmentation of society such as the breaking up of family; *technoplosion* or the proliferation of gadgets and appliances that can influence society for good or evil. The accelerated speed at which things are being devised and produced has given rise to the "throwaway economy" and the "throwaway culture." Thus we have throwaway plates, wedding gowns as well as throwaway marriages, friendships, and partnerships. This easy disposability trend goes hand in hand with the "rental revolution" such as renting of apartments, appliances, jewelry. This eventually leads to the transience of relationships with people; thus we tend to rent "friends," "wives," etc. like objects. Then comes the pressure to hurry up, to adapt quickly to novelty which in turn demands faster but hasty decisions. Decisions, analyses, relationships, and workmanships are made less well, leading to breakdown in performance.

What has management to do in the face of this mounting pressure? Change is life itself. Change must be intelligently managed. It is important that there be balance of change. Man must change proportionally, that is, as he grows physically and technologically, he must grow intellectually, psychologically, spiritually, and morally. Remember what happened during the Industrial Revolution? At that time, men grew rapidly in technology but slowly in moral values. The result was, instead of the machine serving man, man became the slave of the machine. When there is imbalance, the results are catastrophic.

The Ubiquitous Permanence of Change

Change remains feared at, undesirable, and, to many, unmanageable. It is seen as an anathema by those who avoid any encounter with the unknown, the invariable, the unpredictable. For change has always suggested conflict which disturbs stability, peace of mind, and established practices.

Change, however, is everywhere. Developing societies have to face the dilemma of two different value systems (personalistic traditional and impersonalistic modern) competing for the governance of social behavior. In business and industry, many companies would have advertising gimmicks but others do have real product innovations or what they call "product development." This is change. Take the case of some products being advertised in the television such as soap and shampoo products. During the earlier years, these manufacturers were satisfied producing these items for the sole purpose of making the hair clean; but now they produce these items not only for making the hair clean but also making it healthy and as one of the T.V. ad says "to prevent dandruff." Computer machines have also been invented. Even the entertainment field is invaded by these technologies, say the movies with its new sensurround sound; also the service companies with the computerized banks computing interest daily, the fly-now-pay-later plan of travel agencies.

So be it an individual, social group, or business enterprise, there is a continuous change occurring.

The Anatomy of Change

All changes begin in the *environment*. There are aspects of the environment which are relevant to a particular structure or organization and there are those which are not. The *structures* that exist in the relevant environment adapt themselves to the changes and new conditions. This is a must or else the structures become obsolescent and are ultimately destroyed. "Structure" is made up of goals, tasks, resources, relationships, reward-and-punishment systems, communication systems, authority systems. Structural change basically involves *behavioral change* since the net effect of "structure" is a specific set of behavioral patterns. In the human being, however, behavior must be consistent with attitudes. When there is inconsistency, unpleasant tensions arise which the individual seeks to resolve. When he cannot alter his behavior because he cannot leave the structure, he changes his *attitudes* to attain consistency.

In any phenomenon of change or any alteration, there are the *client systems* or recipients of a change element: *system elements* or discrete phenomena that are interrelated and can be considered parts of client systems; *change element* or phenomenon that is foreign to the client system; *change agent* or carrier of a change element; and *resistance to change* or efforts to frustrate or slow the introduction of a change element or to alter its properties.

The Need for Change

In the Philippines, the successful introduction of technological change is often hampered by the rejection of some parts of the change process because these threaten basic value tendencies. Technological change has been successfully integrated with the social system of neighboring countries. They adopt procedures quite different from those in force at the place of origin of the technology, but in keeping with what the culture regards as important.

The Philippines has a long history of contact with other cultures. It has managed to bend and not break even under the strain of violent and imposed contacts.

The Indians in the Philippines

Take the case of the Indians in the Philippines. The advent of the Indian business began in 19th century.[2] The first group of Indians to arrive in the Philippines belonged to Punjabi and Sindhi communities from the west and northwest India. Both these communities are well known for their business skills in India. They came out of India searching for greener pastures. Again around the middle of this century, thousands of them were forced to flee their homes and business when they were rendered refugees during India-Pakistan partition in 1947. Some of them went to the Philippines. Here they completely mingled with the local population, absorbing their culture and habits. Their assimilation was so complete that they came to regard themselves as Filipinos and most of them know about India only as much as the next Filipino does.

Being a business community almost by inheritance, they soon entered into small-time businesses. As these small business enterprises flourished, they gave way to larger department stores. Just as the business prospered, the interrelationship with the local people, who by their very nature are friendly, developed leading to intermarriages. This further led to complete blending. By now, they are all Filipino citizens and Philippines is their motherland, as it should be. They are proudly supporting the Philippines' efforts towards modernization.

The last few years have witnessed the arrival of another kind of Indian businessman—the businessman involved with Philippine-India joint ventures. The Philippines, endowed with rich natural and manpower resources, felt the need for necessary technologies to transform them into productive goods and thus welcomed the assistance of Indian technical experts, particularly in the field of engineering. (India is the third largest pool in the world of technical and scientific personnel.)

The two peoples share a common Asian heritage and both belong to the developing world, struggling and attaining respectable living standards for themselves.

On the cultural aspect, there are numerous similarities as well between the two peoples. They share the same pride in their Asian values, even as they show ambivalence towards western values. This sharing of social and cultural values should, however, be further consolidated by frequent cultural exchanges which, it cannot be denied, have not been up to the required level. It is very essential for fruitful business relations that Indian businessmen first understand the cultural traits of the local people. They must respect their values and sensitively respond to their sentiments. A neglect of these aspects could lead to misunderstanding and suspicion. Filipinos are a very proud and sensitive people and they will never bargain their values for anything.

The development of Philippine-Indian joint venture will see more favorable implications for their mutual trade relations. As it is, the Philippines has undoubtedly the best managerial talent in one of the most rapidly developing parts of the world, that is, Southeast Asia. A combination of Indian technical expertise and Filipino managerial expertise to operate projects in the third world countries could be another favorable result of the mutual business relations between the two countries.

The Chinese in the Philippines

The Chinese in the Philippines originate mostly from Fookien where during one 220-year period, famine swept the land once every eleven years. Their values were focused in nature. The local Chinese, later, were forced out from farming and the professionals to business. Thus we have Chinese proverbs like "once you have money, it is easy to talk" and "busy hands keep poverty away." Such values emphasize diligence, explaining the Chinese attitude to the more easy-going Filipinos around them.

The Chinese know how to share their wealth. They respond generously to appeals for relief funds when disaster occurs. Chinese names appear often in the newspaper list of donors; and they give sizeable sums in such emergencies. Popularity for them is not based on conspicuous spending like extra cars and stylish living.

Chinese cultural values which are in consonance with Filipino values are family loyalty, *amor propio* (self-respect), *hiya* (sense of shame) and *utang-na-loob* (reciprocity). One of the prime values for the Chinese is filial piety. The almost blind obedience to parents are to the Westerners a thing of utter dependence on elders. But the Chinese think that elders certainly have more experience in living and they have the prerogative to make decisions for their children. Thus the Chinese are erroneously called "yellow race" which connotes cowardice. (Going back to Chinese history, the foreigners called the Chinese "yellow" because whenever a Chinese wanted to intervene or fight for revenge, the elders always got in the way to stop him.)

Values which the Chinese have nurtured through the years are frugality, hard work, and respect for money. The Chinese have the strange habit of saving money until they have enough for spending. They value work as a means to success in the future. Through hard work, they believe man exerts effort and creativity. Respect for money and the things it can buy is held dear by the Chinese. These characteristics are prevalent among Chinese in the Philippines because normally their background is from rags-to-riches. Either because of poverty or material ambitions, Chinese from the mainland emigrated to seek greener pastures. At first, their lives were hard because they had to send a sum of money back to the mainland. Thus, they had to profit as much as possible in order to make ends meet.

From the above exposition of the Indian and Chinese cultures with whom the Philippines is in contact, we can identify two conditions which have to be satisfied for change to take place:

1. The element being introduced has to be perceived as potentially preserving self-esteem and providing prestige;

2. The element being subjected to change has a better chance if it is seen as involving more technical and instrumental steps rather than value revisions. People accept changes which they see as enhancing their status and fulfilling their existing goals. Indeed, the degree of success accorded to any change attempt varies directly with its position on a continuous basis ranging from pure

instrumental to pure basic values and goals; the greater the distance from the basic values end, the greater the chance of success.

Filipino culture provides strong sanctions and of course concomitant rewards to maintain the degree of control it apparently does exercise over individual behavior. The point of leverage then would be to discover the behavior and instrumental acts that will meet the goals set up, without being tangled in the quagmire of deep-seated value commitments. There are two sets of goals that can be simultaneously satisfied: the industrialist can get his workers to behave in ways that are functional to his organizational goals, while the workers satisfy their deeply held value goals, changing their overt behavior, but in response to forces that are seen as consistent with their outlook. This means that actual organizational structure will probably look quite different in the Philippine culture, from the way it looks when the technology was first introduced. In order to reach the goals of industrial change, the Philippines needs only a commitment at first to change behavior by structural relationships in ways that would reinforce important traditional Filipino preferences. When attitudes are consistent with the required behavior, the effect is reinforcement. When they are not, the effect is conflict and tension and "dysfunctional" behavior. It is expected that later the very achievement of these goals will itself motivate the new forms of behavior.

Implications of Filipino Values to Change

A thorough understanding of the implications of Filipino values to change is needed before going through with the discussion. The primary traditional Filipino values are authoritarianism, personalism, and small-group centeredness. These values resulted from the *close family kinship* system existing in the Filipino way of life.

One hears many wonderful things about the Filipino family, and observation indicates that many of these wonderful things are true. In many parts of the Philippines, families stay together almost *regardless* of how the husband and wife feel about each other. It is asserted that potentially disruptious inter-spouse coolness and disrespect might be frequently conceded or at least compensated for by other Filipino cultural forces which push husband

92

and wife together. The first social pressure that makes Filipino marriage "permanent" is the *system of marriage arrangement and surveillance*. In many barrios and small towns (where almost eight out of ten Filipinos live), marriage is decided by the parents and relatives of the bride and groom, for marriage is seen not so much as the joining in matrimony of a couple in love; rather it is an inter-family alliance deliberately entered into for sound economic or other reasons. The alliance is symbolized by the union of a representative couple and sealed by the birth of their first child. The practice of living near one's relatives thus adds a new social pressure favoring the stability of the union: marriage surveillance. Relations are not only interested in the duration of the marriage they planned; they are on hand to *make sure* it works.

Besides social pressure, there is *economic pressure* helping to keep man, wife, and children together. In the rural areas where a typical couple lives, the family forms a functional economic unit. Each member of the family has its own special work-role, and the family that works together has good reason for staying together. A third factor operating to preserve the family group is the *conjugal bond* or the internal sense of obligation and privilege, respect, affection, or sexual attraction existing in the mind and heart of each spouse. This conjugal bond, which may or may not be based in part on a recognition and appreciation of the legal or sacramental marriage contract, is the spouse's personal reason for perseverance. Sometimes, it could consist in a desire to have someone else cook the meals or do the laundry. Thus the "permanence" of family bond in marriage might be held by external compulsion more than internal motivation. There are two points we must emphasize on the implication of the family value with regard change. *First*, the condition of the conjugal bond has always been and will most likely always be a major determinant of the sanity and emotional security of the family members. *Second*, where changes occur to weaken the social and economic pressures which hold the family together, the condition of the conjugal bond may decide not only the happiness of the family members but also the survival of the affected family as a group.

Three processes of change observed in the contemporary Philippines affect tremendously the family values: *centralization, industrialization*, and the *introduction of the concept of romantic love*. Centralization or the shift of people from small to larger settlements means the moving of a couple away from relatives and losing itself in a town or city where it can remain relatively unknown; thus the vigilance of relatives and friends is weakened. Industrialization which causes spatial mobility making families move from town to town and/or city to city for job opportunities weaken to some degree the binding social and economic pressures on the affected families. Romantic love or complete disregard of mature deliberation and parental advice makes marriage and family life void of emotional and financial investments.

The importance of the family value is more emphasized if we consider that the basic building blocks of Philippine social organization are the *elementary* family which includes the father, mother, and children; and the *bilateral extended* family which embraces all relatives of the father and mother. Philippine social organization may be characterized as familial. The persuasive influence of the family upon all segments of Philippine social organizations can be illustrated in many ways. Religious responsibility, for example, is familial rather than church-centered. The influence of the family upon economic and entrepreneurial activities is also great. The elementary family is the basic production unit in agricultural activities, and the so-called "corporations" found in urban areas are generally family holdings.

The Filipino values are most formed in the individual in his family upbringing where his personality is formed. Sociologists have noted that the Filipino way of life contains inherently contradictory values. The family upbringing acquires a different set of values from what is taught in school. This is obvious in the Filipino outlook towards government, system of justice, professionalism, and even towards himself. The society outside the classroom often presents values and goals that are in conflict with those of the schools. For example, free enterprise capitalism has always emphasized the value of acquiring capital for oneself, while the altruistic ethics taught in schools has always held that giving to others is always better than seeking personal gain. School administrators and educators may be committed to the traditional values, while the students and younger teachers have no roots in the traditional ones; furthermore, they were influenced by the modifications in values relativistic and less individualistic emergent values.

The premise for analyzing Filipino values for some sociologists is that it would be helpful to understand the individual by understanding first the mass. For others, the premise is that individuals first must be studied and on the basis of these studies, it makes sense to study groups and societies; one must never lose sight of the foundation which is the individual itself.

Behavioral Problems and Change

The manager holds a key role in bringing about change. One of the basic elements of the systematic model of organizations is the notion that the manager cannot stand apart from his workers and try to influence them by remote control. If he tries this game, the workers have much more potent ammunition to throw at him than he can master by using his formal authority alone. The manager's perceptions, value system which may promulgate all manners of rules and regulations—as well as his interpersonal behavior—are part of the system that workers are responding to.

Following this line of reasoning, a promising starting point for the manager contemplating change would be his own behavior. Indeed, in the long run, the manager has a much better chance of introducing change successfully if he can realistically assess the nature of the relationship between his own behavior and the response of the workers. In the Philippines, the manager who is involved with his workers does not have at his disposal the very forces that so often act to dissipate his best-planned initiatives. The workers he has to deal with already possess the potential for strong loyalty, group solidarity, the necessary and effective sanctions for monitoring conformity, respect towards appropriate figures and enormous fears of being shamed.

The change under consideration is a planned change which is a deliberate and collaborative process involving a change agent and a client system which are brought together to solve a problem; more generally, to plan and attain an improved state of functioning in the client system by utilizing and applying valid knowledge.

The behavioral factors that must be considered in planned change are: behavior of person operating within specific institutional environment; interrelated levels (person, role, groups, larger organization); variables that the policy maker and practitioner can understand, manipulate, and evaluate; selection of variable most appropriate to a specific planned change in terms of its own values, ethics, and moralities; acknowledgment of premise that groups and organizations as units are amenable to; empirical and analytical treatment of the individual; social process of change as well as the interpersonal aspects of the collaborative process; and propositions susceptible to empirical test focusing on the dynamics of change.

There are practical cases based on experience of local companies in the Philippines that have undergone certain changes lest the old order drag the enterprise down, and of those that have anticipated change to prevent a problematic situation characterized by stagnation.

Take the case involving a merger of two companies engaged in telecommunication.[3] One telecommunication company, operating limitedly within the confines of its franchise, merged with another company operating a similar business but with a larger and more auspicious franchise, in order to expand. In the process, the name of the larger company was used as the corporate name of the merger.

In that particular case, the planned change is the process that led to the merger; the change element is the name and entities of the larger company used as the corporate name of the merger and other entities introduced; the client system is the original company; and the change agents are the owners of both companies that formed the merger.

Although the merger was conceived under a planned change for a longer and more viable operation of the client system, the element of change introduced by the agent of change brought about feelings of insecurities in the client system. The employees belonging to the client system felt insecure in their jobs when they learned that the name of the other company was used as the corporate name of the merger. This insecurity was largely due to their belief that such a change element would have the following repercussions:

(1) That the other company would eventually take over the merger and institute organizational change that might threaten or jeopardize their positions. (The value involved is *pagmamayari* or the tendency to place a high regard for profession and attainment.);

(2) That there might be more detrimental policies in the other company that might be applied to them when that company should prevail in the merger. (The value involved is *lamangan* or the tendency to feel good after putting one over another.);

(3) That the ensuing reorganization might dismantle old inter-office relationships. (The values involved are *pakikisama* or the tendency to behave as part of a group such that the individual is obligated to that group, and *bata-bata* system or patron-client relationship.)

Before the widespread apprehension could develop into a crisis, the central management of the client system was able to move into activating the members of the client system to be receptive to change. All levels of management were mobilized to conduct person-to-person communication with their subordinates for prompt relief of anxiety. This was followed by personal contacts of senior executives with various groups of employees to convey optimism and conviction that the assurances made by their immediate managers and supervisors reflect top management's thinking and direction. Periodic meetings were held about the immediate and long-range plans of the company to completely drop the *bahala na* attitude of certain individual employees and work groups still harboring some reservations. Thereafter, the employees began to recognize the rationale of the merger.

Another case is that of a shipping company.[4] A large number of cargo handlers were employed by a shipping company for its break-bulk system of cargo handling. The break-bulk system is unwieldy and tedious because it is a piece-by-piece handling of cargo. It is expensive on labor and time.

To solve this operational deficiency, the shipping company introduced the containerization system. This involves the handling of cargo in bulk inside containerized vans. This would incur bigger investment but would turn out profitable for the company in the long run. The new technology in cargo handling introduced by the shipping company would require substantial retrenchment in workers. At the inception of this system, grumbling of discontent was already overheard as the fear of imminent lay-off struck the workers. Nevertheless, top management of the shipping company relieved their fears by proper management of change as follows:

(1) The promising workers were trained to handle the equipment and tools for the containerization system.
(2) Some were assigned for other utility jobs within the shipping company.
(3) Management explored the possibilities of relocating a number of the workers for employment in allied companies

whose cargo handling still follows the break-bulk system.
(4) Others were terminated but were given gratuity pay to tide them over probably until they could find another job.

The management of the shipping company realized the psychology of the workers. In order not to encounter problems and troubles in the critical stage of the containerization system with the workers, it allowed a defreezing period before it went full blast into a change. Otherwise, it would ran smack to a lot of untoward reactions that could impede its organizational operations.

A third example of a management of change is the case of one automotive dealership.[5] This dealership carries brand-new car sales, spare parts, and service. One of its marketing strengths was its location which made it accessible to its customers. The number of walk-in customers was high for cars, spare parts, and service by virtue of the dealership's accessibility to the public.

However, due to government road construction program including the construction of superhighways, the number of walk-in prospects and customers went down. As sales dropped, operational efficiency weakened especially in the service shop where morale went down. Mechanics got their incentive from a certain percentage of the excess of their monthly labor sales quota. With this development, it was their apprehension that their attempt at working for incentive would only be an exercise in futility.

Management had already anticipated the government highway construction program that would isolate the trading area and had already planned for a change but due to certain operational constraints the plan was not immediately implemented. But as things went on the management was able to identify the disastrous consequences of inaction so that before the problem could explode into a crisis situation, they embarked upon the task of instituting organizational change and development including the transfer to a new location. This was a difficult task because nowhere could be immediately located a new site in the trading area as big as the original workshop. Chances were the dealership would have to reduce manpower if it decided to settle for a lower operational capacity in a smaller area. Management had qualms in making such a decision to retrench because of its social responsibility.

After identifying the problem and exploring the resources for possible solutions, the management ultimately decided to transfer even to a smaller area provided its location is accessible to customers. To avoid the problem of retrenchment, the management planned to spin-off some of its operations by the formation of satellite workshops. Certain managerial tasks were discentralized to service shop managers and feedback mechanisms were provided by central management for effective operational control.

By instituting organization change and development suitable to the demands of time and circumstances, the company was able to maintain its business perspective in the new order of things without resistance within its ranks.

Characteristics of Philippine Business Organizations

Business organizations regardless of nationality or ownership have similar primary economic reasons for being: to generate profit and to strengthen their financial position. In our treatment of Philippine business organizations, we shall concern ourselves with the behavioral aspects such as the cultural and sociological values and norms and the inherent interpersonal relationship which characterize a greater majority of business entities in the Philippines.

Family-Based Ownership

A cursory evaluation of any listing of business establishments, say the top 1000 corporations in the Philippines, and the exclusion of multinationals from such a list, would eventually lead one to note a general tendency among such entities: they are mainly family-owned companies and in a few instances where there are external equity participation, the share of these outsiders is not so big as to threaten the controlling interest of the holding family. Thus, it is, that we have come to associate major enterprises with their respective controlling families, e.g., San Miguel Corporation and its affiliates with the Sorianos, Manila Bank and subsidiaries with Puyats, Bancofil and company with the Aguirres, the DMG conglomorate group with the Guevaras, Delta Motor Corporation and Silcor companies with the Silverios, the KBS-RPN broadcast empire and its multifaceted investments with the Benedictos, etc., in a very long list of major entities associated with famous, influential and affluent class—whether of the old rich, or the so-called *nouveau riche*. We can therefore safely make the generalization—open of course to very few exceptions—that most Philippine businesses are family-owned and dominated enterprises.

Paternalistic Management Style

The prevalent management style in Philippine business organizations is paternalistic. The original founder of the enterprise, if still active in the management of the business, or his heirs when the pioneering entrepreneur is already inactive—usually runs the business as he would his family, treating his employees as extensions of the class. During the early stages of the business, when the business venture was yet trying to stand on its own feet in the midst of uncertainty, management would tend to be quite shrewd and stingy with benefits—relying instead on the loyalty or pakikisama of the employees during the hard times. At a later, more progressive stage of the business, management would be more generous with those who have shown loyalty to the owners. Depending on the degree of success and the level of security attained by the enterprise, the company would then begin to extend benefits to its employees. For the more affluent institutions, the company would even provide housing facilities for its employees.

Active Family Management

Family-owned enterprises generally always utilize close members of the family as active managers of the business. As a way of acquainting the succeeding generation with the nature of the business, the gifted offsprings or their kins would be made to start in the lower echelons and gradually but inexorably rise through the ranks as understudies of their elders, or of the non-family executives who sooner or later give way to the chosen heirs in running the affairs of the business as a whole, or the particular portion of the business that the family members are assigned to. Almost invariably, the key line positions, especially the post of chief operating officer, or treasurer, are firmly in the hands of the family members. Employees' dealings with family members active in the business as well as those who are simply beneficiaries of the business are important factors in the advancement and growth of such employees within the company. This is not to say that merit is not recognized in Philippine organizations. However, while the value of talent and expertise is rewarded and recognized, the acceptability of the employees to the influential members of the family is essential to any promotion to positions of importance. Conversely, those employees who are not considered "in," or whose loyalty is uncertain are sooner or later weeded out, or they stagnate in their positions in the organization.

100

Formula for Effective Introduction of Change in Philippine Business Organizations

With the prevalence of Philippine cultural values in local business organizations and its closely interlinked family-like structure, the culturally rooted relationship of interdependence serves as the bond between the owners and the workers, the managers and their subordinates.

The first step would be an assessment of the values of the Philippine business organization concerned, with the end-view of redirecting negative values and capitalizing on positive values in the introduction of change.

In initiating change, there are three processes that should be followed. The first process is *unfreezing*, which is the breaking down of mores, customs, and traditions of an individual or group so that he or they be ready to accept new alternatives. The next process is *changing*. Once the individual or group has become motivated to change, he or they are ready to be provided with new patterns of behavior. The third process is *refreezing*, the process by which newly acquired behavior is integrated as patterned behavior into the individual or group's personality or ongoing significant relationships. It is, therefore, necessary to explore all levels by effectively communicating with the organizational members in order to explain the change introduced. In this respect, much of the manager's effects will be directed toward "helping people become aware they have a need they don't know they have." Until this awareness of need is present, change simply will not occur unless it is forced upon the persons in the organization.

One of the more useful techniques and concepts for unfreezing the status quo is the force-field concept developed by Kurt Lewin. According to this concept, any item being attempted to be changed can be located somewhere in a continuum between "more" and "less." The item's specific location in this continuum is that point at which a set of driving forces meet a set of restraining forces, that is, the point at which these two sets of forces are counterbalanced. The key is in identifying all possible restraining and driving forces. Usually, this is best done at several meetings and by involving all pertinent persons who have knowledge of possible relevant forces. The next step is to somehow weigh the strength of each of the forces and see to it that the restraining forces can be converted to driving forces. Once these factors are assured, execute the change gradually to allow the persons in the organization some period of adjustment and systematically in order that change element can be appreciated by them in its right perspective. Whenever possible, involve people in the organization in planning and decisions that affect them directly or which they will have to implement. Provide feedback opportunities so persons in the organization can air their opposition and feelings about the proposed change. Be considerate of group standards, norms, and habits. Be very certain that employees fully understand the objectives and goals of the change. If possible, try out the change effort in a small part of the organization and introduce the change in phases rather than all at once. See to it that a feedback mechanism is installed as basis for evaluation of the situation and make a follow through to stabilize change.

REFERENCE NOTES

[1]Sebastian Cataroja, "The Permanence of Change," *Philippine Panorama* (December 15, 1974), p. 9.

[2]Pradyuet Madhab, "Indian Business Venture in the Philippines." (A Paper submitted for Partial Fulfillment of the Course Administrative Process and Organization Behavior, Ateneo Graduate School of Business, 1979), p. 1.

[3]Ciriaco Cruz, et al. "Behavioral Problems in Introducing Change in Philippine Business Organization." (A term paper submitted to Ateneo Graduate School of Business, 1979), p. 12.

[4]Ibid., p. 14.

[5]Ibid., p. 16.

Towards a Synthesis of Filipino Values

The Filipino today, in his attempt to modernize and develop, is faced with a two-fold endeavor: to curve his national identity and to cope with the never-ending change. Experience has taught him that institutions, systems, and values copied from western models do not operate effectively in the Philippines as they do in their original setting. Management models built on the basis of foreign experience, if not modified or adapted, can result in negative effects. The Filipino himself is at a lost because of the impact of several values, sometimes conflicting ones, in his heart, mind, lifestyle, and management style. Such a phenomenon demands for a Filipino values synthesis.

Is There a Filipino Culture?

The Filipinos are invariably described as either Occidental or Oriental, or a hybrid of both. From this, some authors argue that the Filipino is basically Spanish and/or Latin; one American author affirmed that 50 percent of Filipino lifeways is American. Waves of migration and external influences are said to have shaped the Filipino culture and society. Everything seems to be borrowed, ready-made.

Culture is defined as the common learned way of life of a society which is reflected in its customs, traditions, folkways, mores, and beliefs as well as in the totality of tools, techniques, artifacts, etc., that are used or practised by the people in it. Values, attitudes, and norms are also part of culture. *Values* are the

103

things considered good, important, and desirable in life. The family, the school, and other social agents are the channels or conveyors of values and ideals which an individual learns to accept through cultural conditioning. *Norms* are the standards of behavior prescribed by society for its members to follow. They determine how people should behave in accordance with sex, age, socioeconomic status, occupation, etc. *Attitudes* are orientations toward or away from some objects, concepts, or situations, and a readiness to respond in a predetermined manner to these or related objects, concepts, or situations. The formation of attitudes may be attributed to such factors as culture, the home and family within a culture, and the individual's social interactions with formal and informal groups. Attitudes are, in part, determined by the culture in which the individual is reared.

From this definition of culture, we can affirm that there is a distinct and unique Filipino culture and society. If we compare the basic institutional features of the many cultural-linguistic groups in the Philippines, we will find a fundamental and distinctive sameness everywhere: in the structure of the family and kin-groups which reckons relationship *bilaterally;* in the organization of society into horizontally distinct generations, supporting a powerful pattern of generational respect which shapes interpersonal relationships, in' leadership based upon wealth, size of the supporting kinship group, personality qualities and age; in economic activities; in traditional religious beliefs and so on. Furthermore, there are only eight cultural-linguistic groups in the Philippines wherein 90 percent of the Filipinos belong. Moreover, these eight groups still show greater similarity in their cultural and social organizations. They have shared common prehistoric and historical influences and made parallel adjustments to a relatively uniform, lowland environment. It is also believed that all languages of the Philippines descend from a single prototype. It is merely the economic factors such as land usage and type, supported by ethnocentrism built upon linguistic isolation, which cause the local or regional distinctiveness in the Philippines.

It was during the pre-Spanish times that the basic features of contemporary Filipino culture and society such as the family, kinship, leadership, social class, economic behavior, concepts of causation theories of disease, patterns of interpersonal relationships were developed. The Spanish and American external influences added many features to Filipino culture and society.

However, these influences were adapted to and modified by existing traditions and social arrangements. For example, the formal god-parenthood system as it works in Filipino society arrangements has an *added function* in ritual extension kinship. The Filipinos are Christian; basically Catholic in affiliation, but *folk Catholic* in practice.

The contemporary configuration of Filipino culture and society continues to mold and adapt economic and cultural external influences to a matrix which in its totality is Filipino or becomes Filipino. By historical accident, the Filipino has chosen the Occident as his image of social and economic progress. However, if he continues to enjoy the freedom of choice and association, the results of future external influences will strengthen, not diminish, the uniqueness of Filipino culture and society.

There exists a Filipino "world-view"—a cultural "whole" of social arrangements integrated in values and beliefs, as well as patterns of interpersonal behavior—which provides a positive definition of what is desirable and undesirable, worth doing and not worth doing.

Acceptance of Western Value System

A casual observer of Philippine society finds that the evidence of the acceptance of western values is overwhelming. Here is the only predominantly Christian country in the orient, a country where western garb has become a standard of fashion, where democracy has come to seem a natural type of governmental organization, where golf and basketball are major pastimes, where no cost is too great for a college degree, and where imported mass-produced products flood the markets.

Those hundred years of Spanish rule followed by nearly a half century of American tutelage have left an indelible stamp of western culture on the Filipino life. Jacoby distinguishes the Philippines from the rest of Asia as follows:[1]

For the spiritual development of the Filipinos, however, American influence in education becomes of decisive importance. The American creed of equality and liberty, and the confidence in progress and in a high standard of living for everybody, have changed the Filipino. He feels different from his ancestor and has accepted Western ideology and ways of thinking, not as an additional

105

attribute, but also as an inherited right. This process of mental assimilation cannot be emphasized too strongly.

Spain played the greatest role in the diffusion of western culture. Spain transmitted religion, technical skills, family patterns, governmental organization, language, cuisine, and many other types of cultural traits and patterns.

Selectively assimilated elements from Spanish and American cultures compose the Filipino's occidentalism. Spain emphasized the spiritual aspects of life, the improvement of the colonized Filipino in preparation for life after death. Thus, she set the foundation for the present Filipino's inclination to denominational membership, anti-divorce control legislations, fiesta and ceremony, tolerance of gambling along with charitable activities, and the faithful attendance at mass and the confessional.

The Americanization of the Filipino consisted mainly of the secularization of life, that is, the improvement of the conditions of the colonized Filipino. She introduced the democratic government with features like bill of rights, the supremacy of the constitution, representative government, popular election, a relatively nonpolitical civil service, free public school system, English language, religious freedom and many other American social norms of thinking.

America left imprints on the Filipino cultural heritage. She inculcated in the Filipino a high regard for formal certification of learning through a pattern of universal education, thus popularizing education as the most essential channel for social mobility in Philippine society, intensifying the Filipino's preference for academic white-collar occupations, increasing the significance of the use of honorific titles, and ushering in the tolerance of "diploma mill" practices.

Secondary means of communication brought over other western influences such as the secular orientation of the French Enlightenment from which many Filipino revolutionary thinkers and heroes drew inspiration and the romanticism of the literary, musical, and other arts.

More recently the Filipino has been exposed to even more conflicting cultural elements channel through mass education, mass media of communication, educational exchange programs, economic and diplomatic exchange missions, religious pilgrimages and missionary work, socioeconomic developmental programs, and increased internal and external migrations.

106

Foundations on Oriental Value Systems

Aeta, Indonesian, Malayan, Hindu, Arabian, and Chinese elements are the foundations of the Filipino orientation and the core of his moral and social conscience, and cultural identity. This orientation is generally characterized by interpersonal and social relationships around blood ties, marriage, ritual kinship, shared residence, common interests and experiences, and community level ritual organizations which are deeply rooted in the soil and sea.

In spite of the Filipino's acceptance of western value system, Philippine society has remained by and large a *bayanihan* society with a tendency to stress tradition, authority, personalism, family ties, interdependence, and harmony rather than innovation, autonomy, and achievement. The bayanihan society tends to stress the importance of group rather than individual, shame rather than guilt, the particularistic rather than the universal, and the acceptance of fate rather than the demand to remake the world.

The underlying values of the Oriental Filipino, his basic temperament and outlook, his patterns of behavior and belief-systems have persisted because the changes which have occurred within the historical period, due largely to western influences, have been adapted to local patterns of doing, believing, and thinking. Historically, most of the values often referred to as western have developed in a *gesellschaft* (urban) type of society. It is in the industrialized, impersonal, rationalistic culture that values of efficiency, time consciousness, innovation, universalism, individualism, and future planning orientation develop. The Filipino orientation has caused the modification of western culture regardless of its mode of presentation or its source of origin. The result is that organizations copied after western models do not operate in exactly the same way in the Philippines as they do in their original setting. Governmental, educational, and medical institutions are largely built on the basis of American models yet they do not function in exactly the same way. In the United States, it is "you ask for it, you got it"; in the Philippines, however, it is "you ask for it, forget it." Business concerns are apt to be operated either by aliens or by Filipinos who have had an unusual degree of exposure to alien culture. On the other hand, a western education in a foreign setting still enjoys great prestige but the Filipino who graduates from an American university is likely to find his newly acquired skills inoperative in his own society. Most likely, his western skills would be rejected and his ambitions blocked in his own homeland where reciprocity and smooth interpersonal relationships are more important rather than efficiency and objectivity. In summary, western gesellschaft cultural values have high prestige but bayanihan values have not been displaced and the result is a conflicting, negative combination of antagonistic elements rather than a safe and sound synthesis of values.

The Philippine Society

The Philippines, largely as a result of an historical accident, has chosen the West as its image of social and economic progress. However, there is a Filipino society with its own view of a cultural "whole" of social arrangements integrated with values and beliefs, as well as patterns of interpersonal behavior, which provides a *positive* definition of what is desirable and undesirable, worth doing and not worth doing.

From the point of view of statistics, 90 percent of the Philippine wealth belongs to 10 percent of the population, which means that the remaining 90 percent comprises the poor people. There is a new upper class Filipino, representing what has emerged as "Filipino" but imbued with essentially the same values found in the old Spanish society—the ownership of land seen as the ultimate criterion of status, avoiding all forms of manual labor, and supporting a closed class system in which there is a wide gap between the rich and the poor.

A Matriarchal Society

The Philippines is run by women, and the Filipino male let them. Even during pre-Hispanic period, the Filipino woman was pretty much the head of the house for the husband was out most of the time busy as a warrior. This fact is strengthened by the Filipino phrase *under the saya* to depict the truth that it is the woman who governs the home, and does govern also society. Unlike some European and Oriental customs, courtship and marriage rituals are in favor of the woman. The groom has to pay his future father-in-law a dowry or "bride price" or had to perform some service for free for a certain period in his father-in-law's house.[2] The Filipina has more rights than her counterparts in other countries in Asia, even before the coming of the Spaniards. Some random surveys indicate that it is the women who do the buying. This is because she as *kabiyak ng puso at kabiyak ng pitaka* manages the purse at home and by virtue of this acquires a measure of power in business affairs. She is a dominant force not only in the home but in the office and most fields of endeavor. She is so literate and intelligent that she knows how to swoon prettily, to drop handkerchiefs and eyelids effectively, and to appear dependent and naive. Thus, the Filipino saying "Ladies first! "

Since the Filipino woman won her suffrage rights in 1937, she has shown an aggressiveness in the pursuit and practice of professions and occupations that have taken her out of the confines of the home.[3] There are prominent Filipino women who are public figures, personnel managers, university department heads, justices of the peace, factory quality control officers, architects, physicians, and professors. In spite all these, officially, women in the Philippines are given no direct hand in formal organizations. They are considered as adjuncts, associates, assistants, auxiliaries.

Filipino women must be permitted to play an important role in society. We can enhance society by improving "womanpower." If this is not done so, female potential for productivity is wasted. They have their share in societal development. To educate society, we must educate the women.

The Filipino family through the woman (wife, daughter, or maid) must be taught to recognize basic needs instead of artificial needs created by advertisements. They must be given guidance in wise buying. They should be taught to maintain equilibrium in buying. As consumers, women have not fully learned their rights and responsibilities. They still indulge in panic-buying and hoarding, disrupting the economy. This attitude may be due to lack of consumer education, *hiya* or "let others-take-care-of-it attitude."

The Filipino woman should learn to maintain a balance between responsibilities to the home and society. Filipino values still reaffirm that the family is a very important institution and we must therefore maintain its strength.

The Family: A Basic Structural Feature of Filipino Society

One author described the larger Filipino society as the anarchy of families. Thus, the importance of analyzing the Filipino family as one of the basic structural features of Filipino society, aside from the sibling group, the large network of social relationships expanded by the mechanism of kinship or quasi-kinship, the two-class system (an emerging middle class in urban areas) and the horizontal separation of the society into distinct generations.

The Filipino family is a highly centralized unit demanding the interest and loyalty of its members to the exclusion of the broader units of society. The Filipino is taught from childhood that his primary loyalty belongs to the family. Since he sees himself as an integral part of the family, his self-esteem rises and falls with that of the family members. The success or disgrace of one member is felt by all.

Furthermore, it is the kinship group that serves as the individual's additional means of contact with the outside world. Interpersonal and intergroup movements of people in and out are largely determined by kinship. Group alliances are likewise formed on this basis. For instance, if a co-member has been insulted by an outside group's member, it becomes the in-group's responsibility to avenge for that collective insult.

Filipino kinship is characterized as bilateral in the sense that there is not, as in lineal or clan systems, a structural bias favoring either the mother's or father's. It is also extended in that each individual has obligations not only to parents and siblings, but to cousins as well. He is expected to obey and respect his parents, older brothers and sisters, grandparents, uncles and aunts. This includes the use of respect terms such as *po, ho, ate, kuya*, etc. and a deferential manner in communication.

Accordingly, a Filipino has many relatives with whom help may be exchanged in the form of money, food, or contacts. However, the immediate family is usually more important than other blood relatives, or the *kamag-anak*. While obligations are enforced in various ways, there is a more limited tradition of concern for non-kin and for the abstract common good.

The family is seen as providing an outlet for the need of a person to get out of himself and come into contact with another person in a free and unguarded emotional exchange. The family exists as some kind of security blanket which protects its members, whether right or wrong. It provides understanding, acceptance, a place where, no matter how far or how wrongly one has wandered, he can always return. The family is also viewed as a defense against a potentially hostile world, as insurance against hunger and old age, as a place where one can be himself without

110

having to worry too much about maintaining smooth interpersonal relationship.

This value, by far, is the largest area in the total field of values where the family is seen *as an end in itself,* without need of subordinating it to other values. Take the case where a parent would do anything just so he can be with his only child who happens to be abroad.

The common themes reechoing this value are:

1. The interest of the individual must be sacrificed for the good of the family.
   a. Parents must strive, even at great costs to themselves, to give their children education.
   b. Older children must make sacrifices for younger children.
   c. Even marriages must, at times, be put off to help the family.
   d. Mothers, especially, must sacrifice themselves for the family.
2. Parents should be very strict in watching over, protecting, and curbing their children who might otherwise meet a disaster.
   a. Physical harm may befall the child.
   b. If left to themselves, moral harm will befall the children, especially the girls.
   c. There is fear that when children leave the house, they may meet an accident.
   d. Somehow or the other, even this bodily protectiveness, over which there is so much concern, is linked to the drive for family security.
3. Women are highly valued for their qualities as mothers and housekeepers.
   a. Women are to be dedicated to the children, the church, and the kitchen or housekeeping.
   b. Women are undemanding. They love one and only one.
   c. A marriage should be kept intact no matter what the husband might do. The women should forgive an unfaithful husband.
   d. Away from the family, women are insecure and worry about losing their chastity.
4. Tender relationships, *cariño* and *lambingan* are highly prized. Oftentimes, there is a sad, nostalgic note. Memories of close relationships are sweeter.

a. Husband and wife are close to each other. The wife pleads for her son.

b. Even in his delirium, a man thinks of his loved ones.

c. A husband parts with pain from his wife. He leaves her with her parents.

d. A girl, jilted, seeks comfort from her mother.

e. Marrying a Filipino is preferred than to a foreigner.

5. In order that the family may remain close and secure, someone must exert firm authority.

a. A daughter is strictly disciplined so that she can finish a career, earn money, and help support the other children. The hierarchy of means and ends is noteworthy.

b. A grandmother wishes to keep the children together by keeping the property together.

c. Children may marry only with the consent of the parents; even when they elope, there must be a reconciliation with the parents. Without such reconciliation, there is great fear that the marriage will not be a success.

d. The parents are expected to tolerate their children's choices and to forgive them if they elope.

e. There is a tendency to marry even against their parents' wishes especially among educated children.

6. Authority figures must be respected and obeyed, though only within limits.

a. A person must heed parental advice.

b. It is the thought of the masters that makes their subjects behave even in their absence.

c. Since mothers influence the marriage choices of their daughters, it is also good to court the mother.

d. It is for a person to keep quiet when scolded and to think things out for himself.

e. Parental cruelty gives the child the right to run away.

f. Authority figures are feared and served with awe but are sometimes not really loved. When they lose their authority, the real feelings of others towards them become manifest.

7. One looks to authority figures for help in obtaining a job and other benefits.

a. It is good to establish good relations with a tycoon or a manager.

b. Benefits come by way of patronage and gifts.

8. Tradition must be followed. The form of authority, especially that of age, so dominates the individual that he refuses to let go of the group's accepted norms. The individual must not rise above the group; otherwise, social pressure will try to pull him down to the level of everyone else.

    a. A man's children till the same land as their fathers did.

    b. One works for success in the city so as to be able to return to the town he left without shame.

    c. One must be on guard against strangers and innovators who may bring reform to the family's traditional way of life. One must please them, i.e., one must be careful about SIR (Smooth Interpersonal Relationship).

    d. The authority figure must be followed even when insisting old-fashioned ideas.

9. One must be careful about what the neighbors are thinking regarding oneself.

    a. Parents teach their family to behave so that they will be appreciated and respected by the community and also for morality's sake.

10. Everyone should strive to obtain economic sufficiency for the family. It is most often a desire to raise the standard of living of one's family or of one's hometown as a repayment for one's debt of gratitude to parents and relatives. It is rarely that the value is expressed as a desire for individual success to make good one's character.

    a. A man's successful business is associated with a happy family.

    b. Even the wife is expected to do her bit in the family finances.

    c. Stealing is sometimes condoned to keep the family alive.

11. One must study and work hard to improve one's economic condition.

12. Social recognition is a major aim in attending school and getting a job.

    a. A diploma is a means to prestige.

    b. Success is associated with recognition by important people.

13. The woman is expected to suffer in silence. A person must suffer before gaining happiness. Patience, suffering, and endurance appear when the frustrating force is conceived as too powerful to overcome. This value has become fused with the religious value be-

cause it seems that God is called upon when other means fail. Sometimes, this value appears with a certain magical quality about it, as if one were to render oneself worthy of divine blessing simply by being patient

    a. The woman endures her husband's grumbling.

    b. The woman takes refuge in religion and music.

14. Children are highly valued as a source of family strength and stability and as a form of old age insurance. *Ang anak ay kayamanan* (Children are wealth).

15. Filipinos are deeply conscious of the status they occupy in society. They regard themselves as rich or poor, *malakas* or *mahina*, class or *bakya*, etc. Status consciousness guides his behavior and determines the nature of his personality and capacity in relation to the state of the person or the group with whom he interacts. To a Filipino, one's house is a status symbol. The house must be at its best (floor waxed, walls scrubbed, new curtains, etc.) before it can be considered worthy of company. This self-consciousness becomes even greater when a foreign visitor or someone higher in class status is involved. Even after a thorough cleaning of his house, he would still apologize for it *(Pagpasensiyahan po ninyo ang bahay namin).*

16. The Filipino has fear of solitude. Having grown up in a situation dominated by the family, the Filipino experiences a sort of separation anxiety when functioning autonomously. A negative value is placed on solitude so much so that when one finds a person sitting alone, one usually asks what is wrong. From babyhood to death, constant companionship is encouraged so that Philippine society looks with downright disapproval on certain norms of independent behavior.

17. A child is indebted to his parents for his life and is considered ungrateful *(walang utang-na-loob)* if he fails to provide for them in their old age. A common Tagalog saying which shows that gratitude is highly valued in Philippine society runs thus—*Ang hindi lumingon sa pinanggalingan ay hindi makararating sa paroroonan* (He who does not look back to the place he has been to will not get to where he's going).

18. The "sensitiveness" which features interpersonal relationships in Filipino society has its explanation in social relationships and in the absence of highly formal institutional arrangements to govern the *personal* relationships of the kinship world which are extended to the relatively impersonal, non-kinship world. There

exist cultural patterns which have apparently arisen to bridge this social distance. Hospitality, politeness of speech, indirection of interpersonal behavior and so forth are "social bridges."

    a. A spurned lover is told graciously that it is not because he has undesirable qualities that the girl can't marry him. It's simply because the girl feels she's "too young to think of marriage," *wala pa sa loob ko* (literally, "not within me yet," i.e., "I haven't given it a thought"). She insists that they remain good friends so that he will not lose face.

    b. At dances, a girl has to be careful about refusing to dance with a boy she does not like. Such an excuse as "I'm tired" or "I don't know how" must be substantiated, i.e., the girl must be careful to set that particular dance out. Otherwise, it gives the "shamed" man what he considers a legitimate excuse to make trouble. The Tagalog saying *Hindi baleng huwag mo akong mahalin, huwag mo lang akong hiyain* (It does not matter if you don't love me as long as you don't shame me) proves how important it is not to be put to shame.

19. *Machismo* or the belief in male supremacy and the relegation of the women to a secondary or domestic rule is a Filipino value. In organizational interactions, this is negatively manifested as underestimating women's capacity for efficiency and leadership. However, it can also be positively manifested by the *pagpapahalaga sa kababaihan* (the value of placing women in high regard).

Machismo sometimes leads to marital infidelity on the part of the Filipino husband. Although there are no official statistics, it is observed that 90 percent of Filipino husbands are unfaithful.[4] This unfaithfulness is taken lightly (though it must be regarded as serious) and rationalized very frequently. The rationales (excuses) given are: *Hindi tumatanggi ang manok sa palay* (No one refuses a good catch), *Ako'y tao lamang* (I am just human), or *Kaya ko namang i-support sila, eh* (I can support them anyway).

This is where the balance tilts. What ought to be understood as proper sense of values, morality for instance, is encompassed by this Filipino machismo. The double-standard of morality has always been a pain in the ass among Filipino women. In the Philippines, when a girl marries, she has to be a virgin and remain faithful to her husband while the man is free to exercise his sexual rights as he pleases before and during marriage. The Filipino males should be made to realize that manliness does not consist in being

115

able to procreate children and that physical unity is not the be-all in marriage.

Because of machismo, Filipino men are rumored to be Asia's best lovers and this is undisputed. But is he a good father, a responsible husband? This is doubtful. Some practices related to machismo are:

a. *Olog.* This is a communal abode where all marriageable girls in the Igorot village retire after a day's work. But the air is filled with girlish giggles and men's love songs. It is here where girls are wooed and won. Trial marriage between man and woman may follow; and their compatibility is thus determined.

b. *Tuksuhan.* Romance, too, blooms with playful proddings and stolen glances. Intermittent with easy laughter and gentle teasing, love is hinted not by the admirer himself but by his friends and hers. The girl welcomes all this, if she secretly favors him. But he must be quick to get her hints and see beneath her coyness and feigned disinterest, so he can later express his love confidently on his own.

c. *Harana.* Among the island people of Mindoro and the Visayas, songs make the most romantic expression of love; and moonlight meadows provide the ever-romantic setting. The young man, accompanying himself on a guitar, unburdens his feelings in a song. The girl, wakened by his serenade, responds with a song, too, and the singing goes on till they reach an understanding.

d. *Kanda-O-Nga.* Once again, poetry proves its power in winning hearts. But among the Maranaos, it assumes a peculiar, playful form. Man and woman exchange brief love verses called *tubad-tubad* in a shy manner over the shoulders of their go-betweens and do not directly face each other.

e. *Pamamanhikan.* Metaphors are the language of old and yet they have always made for clear and formal understanding as in pamamanhikan, when the man, so to speak, "asks for the woman's hand." Here, in the last and crucial step in the courtship, the elders are brought together and they, in a language so indirect and derived from traditions, manage to settle details of the marriage of their young.

f. *Paninilbihan.* A man sets out to gather and chop wood,

116

fetch water and till her father's farm, if only to win the woman's heart and her family's regard. This is, in fact, the code of courtship among the Tagalogs. It is to prove that even in love, industry and patience have their reward.

Other concepts related to machismo:

a. *Querida System.* Machismo, the double-standard morality and split-level religiosity, has led to the institutionalization of the querida system.[5] This is a way of life wherein a married man maintains a mistress, sometimes to the extent of including a second home. The Filipino married male who keeps a querida provides the mistress subsistence and goes home to her once in a while but he is ever careful to keep the relation secret from his lawful wife. If his mistress bears him a child, he usually supports the illegitimate child but does all precautions not to acknowledge the paternity not only because his wife might discover it but he might be accused of immorality. His position in society, like if he is a government official, also makes him extra careful. This behavior is generally considered "normal" since it goes along with the concept of machismo. It boosts the Filipino male's ego and masculinity. It confers him a prestige and the title *tunay na lalaki.* The general comment is: *lulaki naman, walang mawawala.*

Heavier cultural demands, more rigid norms, and higher expectations from women have shifted the responsibility to the women than to men. The concept is as long as one's wife is not being neglected, Filipino husband is free to go into amatory pursuits. In fact, some generations ago, extramarital affairs were an accepted mode of Filipino married life. It was almost normal for a *padre de familia* to impregnate a young lass in the farm, or a helper who served in the household.[6] The wife was resigned to such a setup. A philandering husband could squander anything on other women while the wife could not dispose of any property, even her own, without her husband's consent.

b. *Pagpapahalaga sa Kababaihan.* If we analyze this value deeper, underlying the pagpapahalaga sa kababaihan or high regard for women is the belief that the woman is a

117

possession of the man. Thus, a woman is enthroned on a pedestal of respectability and at the same time treated as an inferior human being. The Filipina is subordinate to the man. She is useful only as a housewife. She serves well as a decoration. Thus, she is obliged to be beautiful and charming. She is a good object for beauty contests.

The Filipina, as a lawful wife, is required of strict fidelity and chastity. A wife's job is to run the household and raise worthwhile children. Romantic love is not a necessary ingredient of marriage, which is largely functional. A wife is legal, churchly, and permanent. She is the *asawang pambahay*, married in one's youth, skilled in cooking, devoted to mending his socks and to his children as differentiated from the *asawang panlabas*, a woman taken later, prettier, younger, and brought to parties for showing off and in his travels as a companion.

c. *Bawal Kumaliwa.* An automotive salesman has a job that brings him away from home for a long period of time. He has a wife in every town of his assignments. All of them live along his route and he visits them regularly and everyone is happy.

A successful married male executive and equally successful married female executive in Makati find rapport in each other and have periodic sex relations without commitment. Each is happy with his own mate and children and the relationship goes on without disturbing the two families.

A marketing manager of a multi-national company based in Manila had sex with a lovely girl he met in a seminar abroad and who he may never see again.

A married but separated female employee has a sustained relationship with his old married boss she does not love, only because he gives material support to her children by a broken marriage.

A husband buys a house and lot for his mistress in a subdivision in Parañaque. He has attained a reasonable amount of success professionally and economically but not maritally. He has enough money, is getting a little bored with his wife and beginning to feel his youth and his charm slipping away.

The Filipino value of "Bawal Kumaliwa" or "No Left

Turn" has little bearing to the Filipino married men because most of the affairs are classified either as an "affair of rebellion." or an "affair of fulfillment." One is an "affair of rebellion" when the marriage is basically sound but has always failed to satisfy the multi-tintillating and varied needs of the man or has ceased to satisfy him in the wear and tear of time. This is especially true in the case of a frigid, old, cranky, and dilapidated wife. In this case, the husband is in pursuit of romantic courtship, innovative, creative and re-creative playfulness and newness. The higher needs such as emotional security, parenthood, position in the community are adequately met by the marriage. An "affair of fulfillment" is when a husband needs to prove his masculinity such as in the case of childlessness. Another situation would be when the husband is around the age of sixty to seventy but still wants to prove his virility. He simply needs to have an affair to fulfill himself. He would not want to be branded as *supot, baog, binabae,* or *inutil.* He needs to prove *na puede pa.*

d. *Under the saya.* This is a setup wherein the woman assumes superiority over the man in the home. This is the situation where a strong-willed or domineering woman of affluent family marries a weak-willed or condescending husband. There is a shift of family role. The wife grabs the authority and psychologically castrates his husband. Surprisingly, this phenomenon is prevalent in the Philippine setting.

e. *Kursunada.* An intense liking for an object or for a member of the opposite sex. This value brings out the masculine bravado. Sometimes this value connotes a sadistic and lusty fancy when it refers to the opposite condition of intense dislike. If a group of teenagers happens to take fancy of a passerby, this leads to the mauling of the person and the unfortunate fellow is said to be *nakatuwaan.* In the case of a female passerby, it may lead to her being raped. A Filipino may resent the glance of another and strike out in anger.

f. *Tuli or binyagan.* Circumcision or tuli or binyagan is another general practice done to Filipino males. This is the act of cutting off the foreskin of the male genital. Originally, tuli is a sanitary measure in tropical countries but since the penis is regarded as the symbol of masculinity, tuli has become a rite by which a man affirms his supremacy. A Filipino male upon reaching the age of maturity must be circumcised in the Philippine social context or else he is branded as supot, *di-binyagan*, *di-tunay na lalaki*, binabae, or *duwag*.

g. *Primero mano* is the Filipino value which expects unmarried Filipino women to keep their virginity till the day of the marriage ceremony. Filipino males generally place a premium on this supposed virtue. A Filipino male may play around and spend the good life with his cohorts of girls; however, when he decides to settle down, he usually picks out a girl he confirms to be primero mano.

h. *Pakipot*. This is the value which induces Filipino women to play hard-to-get so as to project the modern Maria Clara image. She is to stifle a desire or will in order to put on a good show.

General Filipino Values

1. *The Conscious Past Rather than the Planned Future.* The Philippine society possesses a wealth of traditions concerning ways of work, status prerogatives of individuals, standards of conduct, and the general course of life. In the barrios and provinces, rural people tend to become guardians of such tradition and are therefore opposed to change which may disrupt existing order. Predictions of experts about the future are not the guide to the present societal actuations and activities but the traditions of the past remembered by the elders. Greetings of Filipinos in the rural areas manifest this value. In Tagalog barrios, the response to a greeting would be *Mabuti po naman, katulad ng dati* (Good, Sir, as usual). In Western Visayas, the reply would be *Salamat sa guihapon* (Thank you, as always). All of these connote nothing adverse had happened but in fact there was. The fear of disrupting the existing order makes the Filipino answer this way. Filipinos would tend to hide their real situation to avoid change in the existing order.

2. *Fatalistic Rather than Manipulative Attitudes.* Filipinos tend to regard thoughts, objects, persons, and events as sacred or

as possessed with peculiar virtues and specific spiritual powers and think of them as ends in themselves. For the Filipino, man must adapt himself to nature and to supernatural forces, being under the power of these forces.

Manipulation, on the other hand, implies that man controls his own destiny. He does not accept the caprices of nature but seeks to manipulate nature and his fellowmen to his own benefit. If he fails to prosper, it is not fate but his own poor planning that is responsible. Manipulation is based on rationalism which is reflected in the secularized use of nature and human beings as means through which certain ends are obtained. Underlying this attitude is the belief that by systematic planning, studying, and training, the man can actively control and manipulate his destiny and that he is greatly responsible for plotting his own success or failure.

3. *Authoritarian Rather than Libertarian Norms.* Which is more important, the individual or the group? Should one seek to preserve his own freedom or should he put up with abuse rather than break his loyalty to the group? This question poses the choice between submission to legitimate authority and defense of individual rights.

A study made by an American sociologist, Bartlett Stoodly through distribution of questionnaire on this particular matter to the Filipino youth which was the same questionnaire given to German and American youth, revealed that Filipino and German youth are more inclined to an authoritarian position than the American youth.

4. *Particularistic Rather than Universal Norms.* Particularistic values imply that one's loyalty is to the subgroup of which he is a part. The welfare of the nation, or for that matter, the province or the city, is only incidental. The important consideration is the use of any power the individual gains to strengthen his subgroup. For example, a government official uses his appointive power to give jobs to his friends. Also, the promotion of people who are close to the manager, or the individual comes from the same region as that of the manager. Filipinos do not, at least openly, criticize men in power for favoring their subgroups for this is considered a proper use of power.

This particularistic appeal in the Philippines is deeply rooted in the family and the network of relationships based on the utang-na-loob. One's family obligations often take precedence over everything else. This means not only the immediate family but also collateral relatives, and the extension system of kinship through the compadre system. The family does not exist to serve the larger society but to be served by it. Every member of the family must use his social power to boost the total family group, and non-relatives are only considered insofar as they can advance family interest.

The Philippine Reality

The Philippine reality is a strange phenomenon of national brokenness and individual excellence. This reality is consistent with Philippine history: the downfall of the revolution as a united effort but the individual success and excellence of individual Filipinos.

Today, the individual success and excellence of Filipinos is evident in diverse fields, professions, and disciplines. If we go to politics, we see the same reality. Politics in the Philippines started in tribes and barangays. Before the coming of the Spaniards, barangays were small absolute monarchies confined within large families bound by a need for mutual protection. Each barangay had a leader or a datu, frequently at war with each other over lands, rights, possessions, and duties. Presently, majority of Filipinos often get deeply involved in partisan politics and have come to view political office as the most attractive office to aspire for and the most rewarding endeavor .

Before World War II, the largest landowners held the high positions in the government and wielded power and authority over other members of the community. Campaigns for positions in the government were largely centered on personalities and individual excellence. Power, whether political or economic, is aspired for for individual prestige and aggrandizement. Thus, in politics, the Filipino is a natural dissenter, oppositionist if not subversive, contestant, and non-conformist. When he is politically intoxicated, he is always ready to kick a compatriot, colleague, friend and sometimes even relative.

Man for man, the Filipino is just as good or probably better than any man of other nationality. This is proven by the fact that in the records of the United Nations and UNESCO, the average Filipino college boys and girls in schools and universities abroad do well in research and industrial centers. On this matter Carmen Guerrero-Nakpil writes:[7]

122

When a Filipino is alone in a strange country, or a minority of one, he is brilliant and unstoppable. But his own worst enemy is another Filipino.

It is a common recurrence that when there are two Filipinos in an endeavor or work, each one of them becomes only half as good because he spends half his time fighting the other. The same thing happens when there are three Filipinos; each one is only one-third as good because there's more in fighting.

Why can't Filipinos convert individual excellence into national excellence? Why can't Filipinos galvanize themselves into excellence of a national scale? Why is it so? The following are the factors that give explanation to this phenomenon:

1. *History*

Philippine history shows many examples of individual excellence in whatever regime under whatever circumstances. Lapu-Lapu's individual excellence opened the eyes of the post-Magellan Spaniards, upon learning of the slaying of the circumnavigator in a local dispute, that the thing to do was to sit back and let the "natives" exterminate themselves. During the Spanish colonization, individual excellence in individual revolutions was evident. However, each revolt and local rebellion was put down or betrayed by fellow Filipinos. There were Rizal, del Pilar, Lopez Jaena, the Luna Brothers, Andres Bonifacio, and Emilio Aguinaldo.

The coming of the Americans in the 1900s did not impede the emergence of excellent individuals such as Recto and Laurel. The Americans, however, used the divide-and-rule policy by bringing in Masonry and Protestantism as another religion in contrast to Catholicism, and taught the Filipinos Americanism in contrast to Spanish culture and landlordism.

The Japanese invasion likewise caused the emergence of individual excellence in the heroism of Jose Abad Santos and the unsung heroes of Bataan and Corregidor. Nevertheless, there was the existence of the *makapili*—Filipinos who betrayed their fellow Filipinos to the Japanese authorities leading to their fellowmen's execution.

Postwar Philippines was not different at all. Filipino leadership followed the same direction—individual success. Carmen Guerrero-Nakpil commented that the Filipino public is not a public, but a colorful trough of original individuals, taking pride in being different, disbelieving, changing minds and sides with the whimsy of a tropical typhoon, the unpredictability of peasants and crassness of slum children.[8] Divisiveness is a Filipino malaise and the Filipino has the frivolous talent for intrigue that developed in him the inability to summon unity.

2. *Geography*

The Philippines is by nature fragmented into an archipelago of diversity and for millenia had been disunited by pounding seas and impossible streams of water.

3. *Regionalism*

This is the tendency to emphasize and value, oftentimes to the extremes, the qualities and characteristics of life in a particular region. The Filipino is regionalistic and he thinks only in terms of regional oneness instead of national boundaries. Factionalism and disorganization are the usual results of this value since Filipinos almost always carry this to the extreme.

According to Fr. Bulatao misdirected and excessive regionalism gives rise to many social attitudes which Filipinos should rectify, such as mistrust between co-workers, nepotism, dependency on fellow townmates, graft and corruption, and the fatalistic attitude of the *kababayan* who have fallen into the same rut of misfortune.[9]

The root of regionalism could be traced back to the Spanish era when Filipinos were given positions in the government. This was when the *principalia*, the collection of all the town representatives from the leading families, was formed. Filipinos then would turn to politics and politicians to satisfy their physical, physiological, and even social needs. In turn, the reciprocal favor given them by their representative became dependent on family kinship, ritual kinship, and regionalism. This kind of a relationship resulted to "a highly personal commitment to political leadership."

In the Philippines today, when a Filipino is confronted by the phrase *malakas tayo, eh* as an answer to how somebody got promoted, he readily resigns from asking any further knowing the reality of this condition.

Knowing what being malakas could do, the Filipino tends to adhere more to and patronize family kinship, ritual kinship, and regionalism. The three values, depending on how strong they play on the relationship between individuals, are responsible for the effectivity of being malakas.

It is a fact that Filipinos harbor feelings of dislike among

124

themselves due to their lack of a sense of national unity. Filipinos from different regions speaking different dialects show dislikes and prejudices against one another.

4. Colonial Mentality

One author describes the Filipinos as suffering from "national amnesia" and "colonial mentality." Thus, the Filipino's mania for imported goods and easy adaptation to foreign ideas and ways. The true, the good, and the beautiful to the Filipino is what looks Greek, Sematic, or generally Caucasian. This is also the cause of lack of national integration.

Colonial mentality is the referential use of all things foreign and a dislike for anything local. The Filipino is more likely to use standards from outside his cultural system, standards that *contravene*, even debase his own. Foreign products are praised as superior to local versions. The Filipino is pathetically proud of possessing records that play foreign music, such as American rock operas, that has nothing to do with his cultural traditions.

Psychologically, colonial mentality springs from a certain sense of inferiority. A Filipino does not recognize his own assets; he sees only his liabilities because he has been accustomed to being coaxed and pampered by the luxuries of foreign ways of life. This is because of two wrong attitudes:

(a) *Apathy to one's own.* A mass indifference exists so much so that Filipinos would rather sit idly by than go all the way to see a Filipino play, a local art exhibit, or do things which have direct bearing on his country.
(b) *Idolatry for imported products.* Anything imported is better than locally made.

The *basta local, bulok* thinking thus is very common among many Filipinos. A disdain for local and native values has developed among certain groups which find foreign cultures, ideas, products, systems more attractive.

5. Relax Lang Mentality

Since mother nature has given the Filipino a very benevolent climate without winter which forces people to save, to work hard, to think ahead, and to make use of every minute, he tends to work daily and get things done, with little heed for meeting deadlines or resolving urgent problems.

6. *Filipino Time*

Time is a succession of moments with a starting point and an ending point. For the Filipino, time is a succession of moments without a starting point nor an ending point. He starts when he wants and he ends when he wants. Time for the Filipino is any time; so abundant a commodity that one can waste it away.

7. *Walang Tiwala sa Sarili*

The Filipino, deep inside, suffers from an inferiority complex. He has little faith or trust in himself, as a people pressured by colonial rule for more than three centuries, and tempted to patronize stateside ideals and material goods. He lacks confidence in his own countrymen. He lacks confidence in his own lands, soils, rivers, and forests. It is a contradiction to observe that, for some Filipinos, their own country is not good place to live in while for the Chinese, Japanese, Indian, and even for some Americans and Europeans, the Philippines is a paradise, a Mecca for their souls, and a place where they can make a lot of money.

8. *Compadre System*

The compadre or padrino system is one of the root causes of the Filipino's mediocre accomplishments insofar as contributions to mankind are concerned. Many Filipinos do not exert extraordinary effort in their particular fields of endeavor as they rely so much on the much-abused padrino system and influence peddling to attain their ends.

9. *Walang Bigayan, Walang Lamangan Mentality*

Lamangan is the practice of putting one over on someone. This basically becomes a negative trait in the following manifestations: *palusot*—to take unconventional short cuts to attain objectives or to get away from one's obligations; *lista sa tubig*—to incur debts without any intention of paying back; *naka-isa*—to put one over on another; *kanya-kanya*—to work for one's own group without regard for others; *abuso de confianza*—to abuse a person's goodness, generosity, and trust; *inggit*—to be jealous and disconcerted over another's good fortune to the extent of undermining it; *palakasan*—to use connections with those in power to obtain favors and expedite matters; *dugdag-tawad*—to be dissatisfied with one's just share or to ask for less than what is expected if it is work or responsibility; *lakwatsa*—to play and loaf in the face of responsibilities; *panghikay*—to laugh at the deficiencies of others; *padulas*—the propensity to wrangle a share in another's bounty; *sigurista*—unwillingness to take risks unless one is assured of success.

This trait of putting one over the other negates the principles of brotherhood and equality which underlie the former. In situations of competition, there is the *manlalamang* and the *nalalamangan*. The manlalamang takes advantage of the trust and confidence of the nalalamangan and that results to abuso de confianza. Many times there is no strong social censure on the nanlalamang; instead he is called "wise guy" or smart. His ego is bolstered by this psychological mechanism. The nalamangan on the other hand sometimes seeks revenge.

10. *Tayo-tayo Lamang Mentality*

Sharing is seen in the Filipino way of life but unfortunately it is limited to one's in-group, to which one has personal relationships. Within one's group, sharing is not merely dictated by pressures but it is voluntary. There is justice, charity, love to those who are part of one's group but not to all of society.

11. *Paggalang*

It is respect towards elders and superiors. Elders and superiors are held in such esteem as for the young to entirely lose their resourcefulness, initiative, and creativity. By-products of paggalang are authoritarianism, patriarchalism. A naturally talented Filipino loses his initiative in giving way to an elder brother or to a superior, he remaining unknown in the background. Because of paggalang, much value is given to seniority, rather than to one's ability and skill. One's ability is not freely expressed because of paggalang. One's judgment or opinion, even if objectively better, is silenced in deference to that of the higher figure.

The Filipino's ego is highly in need of security and protection. Possibly as a result of the tender and highly protected upbringing received by the child, the ego seeks to maintain a similar environment as it grows up. It protects itself against the harsh world outside the family by great carefulness; not to take necessary risks (traditionalism), to be careful of what other people would say (hiya), not to antagonize others or create potential enemies (smooth interpersonal relationship), to seek the approval and protection of important people (authoritarianism). It prefers to suffer a loss of goods in patience, since suffering is preferable to insecurity.

12. *Pakikialam*

The tendency of the elders and superiors to be officious and to meddle in the business of their children and subordinates, sometimes under the pretext of guidance and wisdom. As a result of this, the individual cannot innovate nor be creative because pakikialam in the form of dictation impedes his freedom. The younger members of the family are discouraged from participating or airing their views in family affairs, thus not enhancing their ability to develop good judgment, creativity, management, and zeal.

13. *Tungkulin ng Panganay sa Pamilya*

In the Filipino family, the oldest child, who is next in rank to the parents, is expected to act and think like the parents. The care of the younger members of the family and even of the parents in their old age is his responsibility. This value impedes the growth of individual independence; the eldest son's endeavor becomes limited to his own family to the exclusion of the bigger group like the community and the nation. There is very strong family loyalty but weak nationalism and social consciousness.

14. *Pagmamay-ari*

This is the tendency to place a high regard on possession and attainment. Expressed as positive value, this results in thriftiness (i.e., to save money), the tendency to value high education, to value one's home, and to place importance in one's origin or beginning. This trait can also be negatively manifested through selfishness and unwillingness to share one's possessions for the greater interest of one's needy neighbors; the tendency to look after one's own family interest only even to the detriment of the community's interest; the tendency to be tolerant and protective of one's children with the effect of spoiling such children.

15. *Pagkatitulado or Pagpapahalaga sa may Pinag-aralan*

The Filipino feels inadequate if he has not experienced formal education. The compulsion is that he should be schooled to become relevant. *Kahit marunong ka sa buhay, pag wala kang pinag-aralan, api ka pa rin* (Without education, you are abused). Furthermore, the Filipino is very particular about prestige of honorific titles before his name. Society judges one's success in life not in terms of ability and talent but on honorific titles.

Emphasis is given on status rather than function. High status usually imposes both privileges and responsibilities. The privileges are the reward for seeing that a difficult task is performed. A high status person, however, may focus either on the privileges which accompany his position or on the duties he is expected to perform. Similarly, his subordinates may regard him primarily as one gaining privileges or as one who gets a job done.

An example of this type of value judgment is cited in a Filipino agency whose field supervisors reported a need for more adequate transportation. They accordingly assigned automobiles to carry out their field duties. Within a month, however, the field supervisors had lost their automobiles as they had been taken over by top administrators. When a management inspection team discovered this, the cars were handed back to the supervisors, only to show up in the administrators' hands in another month. The problem was finally solved by giving trucks to the supervisors. Since these are not status vehicles, the administrators would not use them and they were allowed to stay with the field supervisors.

This status behavior is seen also in the following examples: an official who feels it is beneath his dignity to leave his desk and go to the field or a top-rated engineer who feels it degrading to sully his hands with manual work. This is not just individual choice since the same values are shared by others as well. One feels that he is risking his status unless he insists on prerogatives that are thought to accompany it.

16. *Ningas Cogon*

This refers to the rapidity with which a new organization may first gather enthusiastic support and then be entirely neglected. Some writers attribute this ningas cogon phenomenon to the dominance of family interest. When powerful members of the family constellation see entry in a new organization as a means of gaining family prestige they move in with all members of the family constellation. A rebuff, frequently in the form of competition for leadership from other family constellations, will cause them to lose interest and the entire family group then becomes inactive. Many corporate groups in the society flourish or fail according to the extent to which they serve the interest of strong family constellation.

Filipinos' productivity is greatly hampered because of this attitude. Numerous projects and business undertakings were lost due to lost of interest on the part of the worker to finish it. Large sums of money and not to mention the man-hours and opportunities are lost because of this attitude.

Due to ningas cogon, the Filipino is not a follow-up people. Filipinos have bright ideas. They market well. They start well. But stop there. They don't follow up.

17. The "Awa" Mentality

Awa (pity, sympathy, supplication, compassion, plea for mercy) is the Filipino value that is much abused, overused, behind which a lot of incompetencies and irregularities are shielded. It is used by employees and officers in the name of charity to overturn established policies and procedures. A government official is bombarded daily by supplications and appeals from all sides such as jobs for the incompetent and inefficient, mercy for the erring and incorrigibles, etc. Nevertheless, there are legitimate cases where awa is invoked in a justified manner such as periods of calamities and national disasters.

18. The Go-between

This serves to prevent a direct quarrel between individuals or groups. He is used to assuage a bruise, heal a wound, or prevent injury. While a westerner would go directly to someone to settle an argument or right a wrong done him, the Filipino would nurse his gripes *(nagtatanim ng galit)* and later on, go to an intermediary, enlist his sympathy, and tell him how he has been wronged or misunderstood. The intermediary plays the role of a sympathetic listener, letting the aggrieved person let off steam, and then helps him cool off by minimizing the slight and asking him to forget it. Later, the go-between goes to the other party, explains the seeming affront, and works hard to effect reconciliation between the two parties. This tendency to refuse to straighten things out or to bring things to a head without the help of an intermediary is due to the desire of the Filipino to avoid direct unpleasantness.

19. Lack of Sportsmanship

This arises from the feeling of disgrace on the part of the loser. There is a tendency to sulk and offer all sorts of excuses for a defeat and to consider it a dishonor. For instance, a Filipino who loses in an election accuses the winner of fraud, cheating, and unfair practices. Ordinarily, he will not cooperate anymore in the endeavors of the winning candidate.

The origin of this trait can be traced down in history. The Spanish colonizers never taught the Filipinos a common language. They only talked about God and His representatives on earth, divine right theory, and blind obedience. The Filipinos did not have a common goal to look for as they could not communicate. Their common goal was God and His power in the friars.

The Spanish government used Filipinos to fight against their fellowmen during rebellions. Spain applied the Roman policy of divide and rule. For instance, Legaspi used Cebuan archers to conquer Raja Soliman's Manila Kingdom. Cebuan archers were also used to suppress Tamblot's revolt in Bohol. Diego Silang's rebellion in Ilocos was quelled by Ibanag, Tinggian, and Igorot warriors; and Ilocano troops were called upon to crush Polaris' revolt in Pangasinan. So up to now there is a never-ending kind of "war" between regional rival blocks.

20. *Mañana Habit*

The mañana habit or procrastination is an example of the indolence of the Filipinos which Rizal wrote about almost a hundred years ago. It is the disposition of staving off responsibility to another day, the tendency to escape from duty and obligation as much as possible. The character Juan Tamad represents this habit, and the much abused phrase *at saka na lang* a vivid illustration of it.

When responsibility can no longer be shaken off and the person is forced to start doing his work, there is a tendency to stop after sometime and discontinue what he has begun. This is called ningas cogon. The essence of this attitude is to start something which one will never finish. Particularly, it is the proneness to leave matters incomplete and unfinished.

21. *The Belief of Filipinos about the Indolence of Filipinos*

Minister Blas Ople in a keynote speech at the 16th National Conference at the Personnel Management Association of the Philippines[10] pointed out that the belief of Filipinos about the indolence of Filipinos is one of the myths in the field of human resources development in the Philippines. The typical Filipino is depicted in the caricature of a Juan Tamad resting in the shade of a guava tree waiting for the fruits to fall.

22. *The Filipino Mentality that the Philippines is such a Small and Insignificant Country*

This is another myth Minister Ople cited, and he argued that if a Filipino conditions himself to being insignificant then he is controlled by that image that he is anyway small, insignificant, and weak, so he might as well let the big guys do the thinking for him. And of course, the big guys will always think of their own interest, not of his, no matter how altruistic they seem to be. So long as the Filipino allows that self-image to control him, to govern him, to circumscribe him he could not emerge from the colonialistic image. He could not extend and widen his horizons in the world.

23. *The Belief that Economic Protectionism is Economic Patriotism*

This is the third myth mentioned by Minister Ople. He affirms that the Philippine economy stagnated because Filipinos never grow out of import substituting strategies. The Filipinos have neglected the countryside in terms of promoting non-agricultural products, small and medium scale industries. The Ranis mission consisting of 32 economists, social scientists coming from many parts of the world, convened in the Philippines and undertook what they thought to be the profoundest examination of the Philippine economy undertaken from the standpoint of human resources. They concluded that the reason why the Philippines does not take off is not because the Filipino managers and the Filipino workers are not proficient, competent, and motivated but because the Philippines insists on overprotecting, pampering, subsidizing inefficient industries. Subsidizing inefficient industry is protecting the inefficient.

24. *Bahala Na*

This is a kind of fatalistic resignation which really represents withdrawal from engagement or crisis or a shirking from personal responsibility. Bahala na works against individual and social progress. The Filipino takes on a posture of resignation to the fact: *Talagang ganyan ang kapalaran*. It harnesses one's behavior to a submissiveness that eats up one's sense of responsibility and personal independence. It provides one with a false sense of self-confidence to proceed with an unsound action in the belief that somehow one will manage to get by. Bahala na influences the Filipino's behavior to the extent of indifference in matters of decisive undertaking. Leaving things to God and His will, one assumes his task with lukewarm responsibility and lame determination. Bahala na may even be blamed for the preoccupation with gambling like *karera* or *sabong;* one has either a winning or losing streak.

25. *Lakad System*

Lakad is derived from the Tagalog term meaning "to walk"—but in Filipino social psychology, it means "to fix things for someone." Often one who wants his appointment papers signed, his salary increased, his business transaction attended to uses this system to get what he wants at the earliest possible time. This lakad complex perpetuates itself, in spite of distaste for it, because it is related with another structured relationship obtaining in the office—public or private—which is the *bata* relationship.

26. *The Bata System*

Bata is a kinship term meaning child. In Filipino social psychology, however, it means a patronized individual, "a protege," "a close friend," "a confidential man," "a loyal comrade," "someone you can call upon in time of need," "a ra-ra boy," and so on. The bata relationship is reciprocal. As in kinship, it carries certain functional rights and obligations—some kind of patterned expectations. In order that a bata relationship can be formed, one of the actors should be in a subordinate position. The structuring of the bata complex becomes clear if we consider the terms the bata uses to address his or her superiors. Functionally, it is clear that kinship is used as the model around which the bata complex is woven.

Filipino Values and Practical Religiosity

Religion would be useless unless man first understands himself in his own time, place, culture, race, and society. It is only when man understands himself, his own limited being, his humble but at the same time rich person, that he will understand religion and his need of it. Real conversion to any religion means first conversion to one's own self.

Split-Level Religiosity in the Filipino

Filipino religiosity is oftentimes termed as split-level religiosity. This is a phenomenon which consists of the coexistence within the same person of two or more thought and behavior systems which are inconsistent with each other. This split-leveling involves the absence of a sense of guilt, or the presence of only a very minimal amount. One who practises a split-level religiosity is convinced that two objectively inconsistent thought and behavior systems really fit each other. This inconsistency is either not perceived at all, or is pushed into the rear portions of consciousness. Hence, the feelings of inconsistency and hypocricy do not arise. This inconsistency remains in the unconscious or in the semi-conscious mind of the person until an authority figure discovers the existence of the split. Accordingly, split-level religiosity sees the need of keeping the authority figure at a distance. This phenomenon is called *distance-making*[11] which is the process of removing the self as far as possible from the gaze of the person in authority who might blame and criticize the ego for consorting with another level. There is the attempt to push the authority figure as far away from oneself as possible.

Reasons for Split-Level Religiosity

Split-level religiosity finds its foundation in the psychological principle that "learning is specific to a situation." A person responds to a particular stimulus, and does not give the same response to another stimulus unless the second stimulus is experienced similarly as the first. So, too, where one set of responses, namely the religious level, is learned within a church or religious setting, and the other set of responses, the pagan or irreligious level, is learned in a street or home setting, and as long as *these two settings are dissimilar*, the two responses will remain specific to their own milieu.

Another cause of split-level religiosity is the distance between the religious authority figure and the home or street setting which sets up two different stimuli-response systems and consequently creates the split-level in the person.

Split-leveling is the practical way the Filipino learns to handle the opposing pressures of two distinct groups holding different value systems. The Filipino, desirous to please two groups possessing opposing value systems, solves the dilemma of both pressures by keeping them apart and by simply ignoring the inconsistencies.

Solution for Split-Level Religiosity

After diagnosis, therapy must be applied. The fact that we, Filipinos, hold on to both levels is an indication that there is some value in both. An interplay between the level coming from religion and the level coming from natural heredity, heritage, and environment may result into something new which will be fully religious and fully Filipino at the same time.

On the social level the religious authority figure must be brought to the people, while on the individual level the religious system of thought and behavior must be allowed to sink into and pervade the whole person taking into consideration his cultural milieu.

Religious Implications of Filipino Values

The Filipino values can serve as the matrix for maximum religiosity of the Filipino. He can develop an authentic and mature religiosity within the context of his own Philippine culture. There are four possible attitudes toward religion. One possible attitude is *not to be aware* that there is religion. Another attitude is *complacency*, when one is aware but not concerned about religion. The third attitude is *timidity*, that is, one considers religion so frightening and difficult that he is afraid to make a commitment. The fourth attitude is *escapism* from religion, avoiding confrontation with the real religious issues in life. People who know they are doing wrong but do not want to change easily rationalize it by such sayings as *ako'y tao lamang, talagang ganyan ang buhay, ganyan naman ang ginagawa ng lahat, ang lagay ba ay sila lamang.*

To impart religious meaning to Filipino values is not a question of authoritative pressure nor of stereotyped instruction, but of understanding, acceptance, and commitment. Religiosity or being religious means a personal and total commitment to religious ideals, principles, and beliefs. Only when a person understands his religious ideals, principles, and beliefs and makes his way of life in accordance to these ideals, principles, and beliefs can we say that he is religious, that he has made a religious commitment. But, before he can commit himself to these religious ideals, he must first be *responsible*, that is, he must be able to respond freely on his own, independent of others; able to think and decide for himself and therefore answerable for his actions. He must accept his status as a free individual person and achieve some personal identity.

135

He must act freely and decisively to become the kind of person he wants himself to be. He must be able to act in response to the call of love for another person. The Filipino, to be able to make religious commitment, must first learn to make a personal, sincere reflection, and a critical self evaluation of his values, culture, tradition, and practices. He must evaluate again his own motivation, form his own moral conscience, and internalize religious ideals, beliefs, and principles on the basis of his values and culture. In this way, religion for the Filipino will become a matter of personal conviction and total commitment rather than a matter of social conformity and force. His religious faith will become for him a religion of interior faith and love rather than a question of merely external rituals such as hearing mass or making *novenas*. Religion will begin to be for the Filipino a matter of personal loyalty to the religious ideals based on his Filipino values. It is only when he has made an integration of his Filipino values and way of life with his religious principles and beliefs that we can say he has achieved real religiosity. The Filipino values can be the potential for his religious renewal. It is a matter of reorienting and mobilizing such values towards the religious beliefs and principles.

The Filipino personalistic values of *ako* or *kami*, if wrongly oriented, may cause disunity inimical to religiosity. It may cause small-group centeredness and hamper spiritual growth and personalism. However, these personalistic values, if directed in the right way, can be a great potential for religious renewal. Genuine personalism is a must for religious maturity. An authentic individualism is a bridge to the understanding and realization of the religious meaning of person, freedom, and love. In the Christian dogma of the Blessed Trinity, we find the mystery of three Persons who freely love one another; and the Trinitarian life is precisely the perfect model of Christian love of God and neighbor. The ako or kami values can be the basis for Christian individualism which should make Christians realize that their faith is not a matter of duty or conformity to social expectations but a matter of a free and personal response of love to God. Religious personalism based on the ako and kami values can be the foundation of love and trust among Filipinos. When the Filipino converts his kami into tayo because of his religious belief in the brotherhood of men and fatherhood of God, the "I—You" relationship becomes the bridge to personal religious commitment to God.

Filipino Values and a Relevant Education

Relevance may be defined as that which responds to felt needs. Conceptual relevance arises in two ways: either it comes from the experience of the people themselves (e.g. hiya, tiyaga, pakikipag-kapuwa-tao) or a foreign concept is brought in and adapted to the local thought-system (e.g. democracy). Bulatao comments:[12]

> The danger of adopting concepts blindly can be disastrous. Take as an example the Ministry of Education's idea of automatic promotions. Even the Ministry of Education admitted that as a result of this policy, 60% of public school 6th graders are functionally illiterate today. The original concept may have been relevant to the U.S. culture and small classes, alert school boards, involved well educated parents. But not in the Philippines where such infrastructure is not present. As for NCEE, how can one run a computer to score the tests when brownouts keep varying and erasing the memory of the computer?

In the process of making an educational concept relevant, the problem in the past has been a lack of emphasis on the built-in cultural difference of the Filipino personality. Not enough attention has been given, in behavioristic terms, to the O variable in the formula Stimulus-Organism-Response. Not enough attention has been paid to the fact that the Filipino organism, the O variable is different. Accordingly, his responses to the educational program itself will be different. In actuality, what he learns in educational institutions is isolated from his experience. There is no integration with actual Philippine reality.

The Myth of Imported Educational Values

For quite a long time educational institutions in the Philippines have been peddling for imported education values from the west. Western concepts and ideas in education have been planned and engineered and then packaged into a curriculum production with a very marketable appeal to the Filipino consumer-pupils. Thus, the Filipino was made to conform to marketable imported values. He was made to believe that the corresponding value of man is measured by his ability to consume and assimilate these western values. In school, he was taught that valuable learning is the result of knowing more "modern" or western concepts and imported ideas; that the value of learning increases with the amount of western input; and, finally, that learning is measured

137

and documented by grades, certificates, and diplomas.

On the contrary, learning is the human activity which needs least manipulation by others. Most learning is the result of unhampered participation in a meaningful setting. The essence of education is that it does not drive people to accept predetermined ends and dictated values, but, instead, fosters the initiative for them to participate intelligently in the choice of ends and values. Learning which significantly influences behavior must be self-appropriated.

The Filipino Learner

According to Deikman's Theory of Bimodal Consciousness in Man, there are the *action* mode and the *receptive* mode in man. The action mode organizes man's consciousness around a person's need to survive and to obtain one's personal goals. Hence, it is rational, attentive to cause and effect, to past and future. In its effort to control reality, its highest achievement is the mastery of words. On the other hand, the receptive mode of consciousness is organized around accepting reality, openness to experience, with attention to now. It is intuitive rather than rational, contemplative rather than actively oriented towards personal objectives. It flows with nature instead of seeking to control or maintain it. Hence, its awareness extends to extrasensory levels of reality and its influence beyond what is easily conceptualized.

The Filipino learner is much more in the receptive mode. For the Filipino, science's effort to control nature and subject it to man's use is hard or difficult to comprehend. He combines insight with reasoning. He must experientially absorb and then express in local concepts, ideas he has assimilated. Thus, education must correspond to the experience of the Filipino. Education will be a realistic and practical guide to life, a source of self-understanding, a map of reality if it is to stimulate him towards human development.

The Filipino learner must be made aware of his own mode of consciousness. The Asian in him brings out the receptive mode. However, we must remember that he has also in himself the dormant western trait—action mode of consciousness. He has both modes; only, the receptive mode is what has surfaced.

Implications to Education of Filipino Values

Education is intended to form the whole man for what he must be and do here below, in order to attain the purpose for which he was created. Filipinos must firstly be educated in his own values for this life and for the life hereafter. Right orientation of natural qualities and values can lead to total development.

Education must first of all be relevant. Its concepts must reflect the Filipino's experience. Its myth, its view on life must be in tune with the Philippine reality. It should make the Filipino understand himself; it should give him a sense of oneness with himself and with his fellow Filipinos. It should help the Filipino identify and pursue his true self-interest. The typical Filipino finds this confusing and difficult. Take the case of a Filipino who just graduated from college, who finds that in spite of his four-year degree, he can't land a job with the salary he demands.

It would be very felicitous to observe that more and more Filipinos are able to acquire certificates and diplomas attesting to their educational standing had it not been for the sad aftermath that the more "educated" a Filipino gets, the more he shies away from manual work. Thus, we hear of many Filipinos who deserted their natural inclination towards farming and agriculture to seek a "white collar" occupation in the cities. Education based on Filipino values must instill in the minds of the Filipino the right attitude towards manual labor and let them realize that in the economy of creation, some are meant to work with their hands, others with their minds.

The Filipino value of *pugkatitulado* (having degree) have made Filipino parents suffer heroic sacrifices to send their children to college, expecting them to secure a lucrative job in the end. Education for Filipinos is a qualification for gainful employment. However, their hopes have oftentimes been dashed to pieces, since it is progressively becoming clear that a mere college or university diploma is not a sure guarantee of employment, much less a lucrative one.

The overemphasis on education as a financial tool has made the Filipino underestimate its humanizing aspects such as the concept of education as a preparation for life on earth, an aid in one's quest for meaning, an openness to truth. Thus, we have the strange phenomena of diploma mills, unskilled technicians and uneducated college graduates.

The Filipino speaks English in multi-regional accents—Ilocano, Pampango, Tagalog, Visayan. The peculiar intonation, vowel and consonant substitutions, grammatical errors, and the mispronunciations the Filipino makes when speaking in English because of

139

the interference of his first language, are some of the over-refinements and educated mistakes of the miseducated Filipino. Morales gives some examples of Filipino English due to the pressure of Tagalog grammatical structures which illustrate this point:[13]

> (1) "I don't like him also." *Hindi ko rin siya gusto* (I don't like him either).
> (2) "I go there already everyday." *Pumupunta na ako doon araw-araw* (I go there everyday).
> (3) "Yes, I'm not going." *Oo, hindi ako pupunta* (No, I'm not going).

English in the Philippines is also afflicted with a great deal of pseudo-refinement. Take the case of the perfectly correct and proper words *pregnancy* and *pregnant* which are generally avoided in favor of *on the way* and *expecting*. *Making love* which means the sexual act is believed by the Filipino to be more harmless than *courting* or *wooing*. When a Filipino says that he "slept *late*," he generally means that he stayed up late.

Perhaps, also a form of circumlocution or at least of polite indirection is the constant use of the progressive form.[14] For example, "I am inviting you to a birthday party next month" in which the invitation is expressed in a state of continuing progress for a long time rather as an explicit quickly completed action. The use of the progressive form among Filipinos is probably due to the fact that it is the verb form most often used in Tagalog or Pilipino. "The First Lady is inviting you" is the Tagalog or Pilipino way of saying 'The First Lady cordially invites you."

The Filipino's tendency to translate a Tagalog idiom into English, word for word makes Filipino English strange. Take the case of a Filipino who wants to compliment a well-dressed American friend by saying that the American "is ready for his funeral" *(nakapamburol—*dressed for his funeral). The American wouldn't understand that what the Filipino meant was the American's "dressed to kill." A Filipino may attribute the promotion of a fellow employee to his having "oiled" *(linangisan)* his boss, that is, he "buttered him up."

Certain social greetings in Filipino when taken literally lead to misunderstanding. The Filipino's usual question of "Where are you going?" *(Saan ka pupunta?)* to an American friend he meets will be very annoying or "nosey" if he does not understand that it is simply the Filipino equivalent for the English "hi" or "hello."

Wanted: Filipino Education

Values have three important functions in education. They are the following:

(1) Integrative function: its role in uniting elements and intitutions of culture.
(2) Its role in providing individual members of society with a purpose or meaning in life.
(3) As the matrix in which human behavior is embedded.

From such functions, we can deduce that education must be well-versed in values for it is the means of transmitting values from one generation to another. Education must be founded on a solid sense and hierarchy of values. Values are the goals of Filipino education, with its purpose to render the Filipino's existence meaningful and for him to achieve the complete fulfillment of his personality as individual and as member of a community. Education in the Philippines must be based on a sound Filipino philosophy of values; science alone is not enough, since its sole business is to describe facts and events, to tell man what happens. It is a Filipino philosophy of values which is concerned with the search for the ultimate *principles*, ultimate *backgrounds* and answer ultimate *questions* about the Filipino. Education must lead the Filipino to the acquisition of right values in life.

The basic and most necessary thing that an educated Filipino should know is the real meaning and purpose of life. He must know why he is alive. From this *knowledge*, he develops *character*, the ability to determine right from wrong and strength to force himself to choose the right. A person, a people, or a nation will be judged as educated by its character. True education pursues the *right goals in life*.

In our country, education must be a vital weapon for our struggle for a national identity, economic independence, and political emancipation. It must produce Filipinos with strong character: Filipinos who have a strong *sense of purpose* and know *the how* of bringing peace, happiness, and abundant well-being. Reexamination of our philosophy, values, and approach in the making of man, in particular of the Filipino, is a must. It is only then we can say that we have a true education which can produce a true Filipino who will institute, support, and lead his country to its proper destiny. We must recapture the true Filipino values of life, the Filipino spirit of righteousness, hospitality, sense of justice, social awareness, sacrifice, and perseverance through education. The making of an educated Filipino is not exactly the same as the making of an educated European or American. Education in the Philippines must be for Filipinos, of Filipinos, and by Filipinos. Our education must be adapted, related, oriented, and attuned to Filipino values.

The Social Values of the Filipinos

The festivals or fiestas are woven deeply into the texture of Filipino life in almost every barrio, town, or city in the Philippines. Though fiestas may be held anytime during the year, the biggest if not the best of them takes place in May, the month between the harvest and the planting when farmers, fishermen and factory workers take a leave from work for a well-earned rest and a bit of merry making.

Farming communities, particularly those in Southern Luzon, honor San Isidro Labrador, the patron saint of farmers, on May 15 with exuberant displays of the fruit of the land. The display called *pahiyas* (decor) are always extravagant, unrestrained. The pahiyas implies that the harvest has been so abundant that ripe rich stalks, bright bunches of bananas, great bean pods, etc. which are plentiful can be used as decoration. If the harvest was abundant, to do less would be considered ungrateful. And if the harvest was lean, the lavish display reminds the saint to do better for the farmers next year.

The greatest number of fiestas, one each day, is celebrated in honor of Mary, Queen of May. There is the *Flores de Mayo* (Flowers of May), a ritual of daily offering of flowers carried by little girls. This is a small, private affair. For some, this is a community-wide ritual, like the evening candlelight processions called *Santa Cruz de Mayo* which commemorate Saint Elena's finding of the Cross on which Christ was crucified. A beauty contest usually accompanies this religious event, since only the town's most beautiful young woman is deemed worthy to portray Saint Elena and only its handsomest young man her son, the Emperor Constantine.

Other fiestas are those held on May 17, 18, and 19 in Obando, Bulacan where elderly women and young wives implore the help of Virgin Mary, Saint Claire, and Saint Pascual to conceive and

142

bear children. In Pakil, Laguna, devotees and singers hop, skip, and leap with joy in procession before a very old picture of the Blessed Mother that when it gets so giddy and frisky it ends with a happy leap into the town's public pool.

Fiesta to the Filipino is leaping for joy. Filipinos don't need an excuse for a fiesta. Almost anything is cause for a celebration— a promotion, passing an examination, recovery from illness, one's first check; in fact, even having a new dress or a new hairdo. All that is needed is for someone to compliment another, say, on how well she looks, and the person complimented would readily say, "Come, I'll give you a blow-out." And of course there are big parties given on big occasions like the baptism of the first child, a daughter's eighteenth birthday, etc. This attitude was existent even before the Spaniards' arrival in the Philippines. Long before the celebrations were called such, Filipinos already enjoyed rousing get-togethers, for any excuse, it seemed. Call it a Malay propensity, a childlike alacrity to celebrate. Call it the perfect response to the rhythm of the seasons. Call it even faith—a conviction that nothing is so bad, it could not be better; that there is always cause for joy.[15] Give a Filipino a reason—any reason—to celebrate and you'll soon have a fiesta in the making.

The fiesta has an immeasurable social value. It is an occasion for getting together, for clans and families to hold reunions. It is a time for demonstrating appreciation—for favors received, for favors done. It is an opportunity for establishing social position, or for redefining it if necessary. It is a chance for paying back debts, not the outright payables, but debts of honor. The fiesta is ulti- mate gesture of respect and esteem, the tangible—yes, digestible— honor. He who does not celebrate is taken to be rude.

The fiesta has also some misdirections though. Less than 20 years ago, a Filipino politician, armed with statistics, shocked people to the lavish expenditures that fiestas entailed, by giving them statistics that equated their celebrations' budget with the profitable investments they could have made in poultry, livestock, or land products. Because of fiestas, Filipinos have become wild drinkers. The fiestas, as celebrated in the Philippines, have more of secular features than religious meaning. Game stalls, ferris wheels, wheel-o-whirls, ago-go dancers and sometimes prostitutes abound during fiesta. Too much money is spent on fiesta. Too much food is eaten during fiesta. Too much wine is drunk during fiesta.

A Filipino value related to fiesta is the Filipino hospitality.

143

Almost all people around the world are hospitable in a way, but the Filipino hospitality is something that is almost to a fault. A Filipino would open his door even to a complete stranger while his foreign counterpart is usually wary and suspicious. He prepares the best food for his guests. If one is caught without food to serve, he hurries to the nearest store to buy food or to the nearest neighbor to borrow some raw meat to be cooked. While cooking he apologizes for the delay and offers his guest something light while in wait. He offers his bed, while he sleeps on the floor and makes you feel that he has been honored by his guests' presence.

Analyzing hospitality, we can see this value being used to achieve social acceptance and smooth interpersonal relationship. During fiesta, extravagant spending is displayed no matter if it buries the host in debt. He avoids *kahihiyan* so he offers the best to his guests.

The Filipino is exuberant in this attitude of uneconomizing. A farmer, for example, would live in utter deprivation for most part of the year and then spend his savings on one big fiesta or celebration.

Serious study should be made on how to make our fiestas lead to progress. Filipinos should be encouraged to spend and use savings for acquiring productive goods and improving their standard of living.

Social Formulas

Let's take the Filipino celebration or party and how the Filipino behaves in it.

(1) A host never knows how many to expect at a party. Not only do the guests not acknowledge invitations, but they also feel free to take along their family and friends. Thus, a party for 20 can easily turn into a party for 40. The host takes this in stride and uninvited guests, nevertheless, are made to feel at home right away. There is no need to worry about food as preparations have been made for twice (or thrice) the number of people expected anyway.

(2) Because it is improper to rush to the dinner table at first call, the host has to go through the painful process of practically pulling everyone to the dinner table.

(3) The host usually does not sit with the guests at the table. Instead, he goes from one guest to another insisting that

144

they try to take more of a certain dish.

(4) There is a tendency for men to sit with men and women to sit with women in parties. A man who joins a women's group is teased for being "a thorn among the roses."

(5) The guest is expected to eat a lot. If he doesn't, the host will feel that his preparations were not good enough. The guest is not supposed to clean up his plate though, unless he wants to give the impression that he is so hungry he has to eat up everything.

(6) Although one doesn't want to invite everyone to a party, a Filipino feels he has to ask everyone casually, otherwise, he has to invite a few friends in secret so that the uninvited will not feel left out. The person invited casually gets the cue when the person inviting him does not insist on his coming.

The Psychology of the Filipino "Yes"

Foreigners and critics of Filipino behavior are oftentimes startled by a positive answer to an appointment or instruction, only to discover later that the same individual did exactly the opposite without cancelling the appointment or asking questions regarding the clarity of the instructions. Below are some situational orientations of a Filipino "yes."

An average Filipino will say "yes" when:

(1) He does not know;
(2) He wants to impress;
(3) He is annoyed;
(4) He wants to end the conversation;
(5) He half-understood the instruction of what is being said;
(6) He is not sure of himself;
(7) He thinks he knows better than the one speaking to him.

A foreigner would not understand why a Filipino says he would try to meet him when he has no intention of doing so. The Filipino simply does not think it right to say he couldn't make it. He thinks he'd save his foreigner friend's feelings that way. The Filipino does not know that this is more annoying to the foreigner not only because he has made the foreigner waste precious time waiting for him but also because the Filipino is not true to his word.

When the Filipino says "I'll try to come," it usually means one of three things:[16]

(1) I can't come, but I don't want to hurt your feelings by saying "no."
(2) I'd like to, but I'm not sure you really want me to come. Please insist that I do.
(3) I'll probably meet you between eight and nine but I'll not say "yes." Something might prevent me from coming.

A foreigner who casually invites a Filipino to dinner must repeat the invitation a second or third time so that the Filipino will be able to distinguish it not as a *pabalat-bunga* (literally, "skin of the fruit," i.e., insincere, casual) invitation but a sincere one.

Usually the Filipino agrees weakly instead of giving a flat refusal of "no." *Siguro nga, Marahil, Pipilitin ko* (Maybe, Perhaps, I'll try) are his usual answers to questions where a foreigner would frankly say "no." This is because of the Filipino's desire to please. To interpret the meaning of his "I'll try" or such similar answers, it requires only a little persuasion to change the vague "I'll try" to a "reluctant yes" or an "apologetic no."

The reluctance to refuse or disagree directly is carried over in discussions. One who differs with a speaker feels that he should not appear to do so. He handles this by saying "Correct me if I am wrong. This is not a criticism. I simply want to clarify certain points. In my own personal opinion . . ." as an introduction to what he wants to say.

This roundabout way of commenting takes place even in supposedly intellectual discussions. Even the most scholarly person cannot escape from feeling that he and his work are one. Thus, a criticism of his work is a criticism of himself as a person. Thus, he reacts to criticisms emotionally unless they are couched in a language that is not hurting.

This also leads to the Filipino's reluctance to ask questions from his teachers and professors. Since they are considered the epitome of wisdom, it is unthinkable for mere students to question them. Besides, a few professors do not encourage questions and consider their position being challenged when students do so. In order to "get along" with such professors, students usually keep quiet and refrain from openly disagreeing with them.

Filipinos sometimes refuse to ask questions because they feel it is *nakakahiya* (shameful) to do so. The popular belief is that only the stupid and the ignorant and the *provinciano* (i.e., the backwoods) ask questions. A Filipino traveller, for instance, would rather get lost looking for an address than ask for information. A worker would rather pretend to understand the instructions given him and risk making a mistake than ask questions.

The right approach for a Filipino if he is to ask question or information is to apologize for it by saying *Mawalang galang na po, maaari po bang magtanong?* (Excuse me, may I ask a question?; literally, May I lose my courtesy? Is it possible to ask?). After receiving the answer or information, the Filipino apologizes for having been a bother.

The Filipino approach in asking someone to do something for him is not to barge in on someone and ask him to do something for him. His preludes to what he wants to say are "Are you busy?" "May I disturb you?" The other from whom favor is requested, even if he is busy, doesn't say so and makes the other person feel that he has all the time for him: *Basta ikaw* (All the time; Anything for you), he would say. In order to facilitate smooth interpersonal relations, great care is taken to avoid giving embarrassment (hiya) to the other person.

Generally the Filipino who calls on a friend specifically to ask for a favor doesn't find the courage to do so until he is almost ready to leave. Then he sees to it that the favor he is asking has the appearance of only an afterthought by saying "Incidentally, I wonder if you can buy a few raffle tickets for our civic organization."

If a Filipino wants to play the role of a perfect host to one who calls to ask for a favor, he anticipates by asking him what he can do for him. And when the caller hesitates, he insists by telling him, *Huwag na kayong mahiya* (Don't be ashamed). So that the person asking for a favor will not be "ashamed" the other party tries not to appear offended. If the favor can not be granted, it's the person who cannot oblige who apologizes for his failure to do so, making it clear that it is not because he does not want to, but there are factors beyond his control which make it impossible for him to oblige at that time. This carefulness not to offend or hurt the petitioner's feelings is such that when one cannot give the favor, such as when a beggar approaches for alms, he asks to be forgiven saying, *patatawarin po.*

Understanding of Filipino Values: A Help to Management

Management definitely can benefit from Filipino values by understanding the behavior of people in the organization. Perceptions, attitudes, and behavior have all been, in large measure, learned from culture. The patterned life experiences of people determine to a large extent these behavior in certain situations. A knowledge of cultural values can enable management to exercise control over its employees.

In the case of a certain production manager whose company has been forced into repeated years of unprofitable operations in an economic atmosphere of increased market competition coupled with escalating product costs, it was discovered that one of the basic problems at the plant was the high and unpredictable rate of employees' absences due to the habit of workers of returning to the province at irregular intervals for a large variety of reasons. This has resulted in delays of production.

Since this company is a family business enterprise, the owners refused to hire workers coming from provinces outside their own. The rationale is to avoid the foundation of unions and to boost the family's election standing when election comes. Because of this hiring policy, the production manager could not get competent men for the job. Even if he were to terminate a worker, the replacement would surely come from the same locale as the former. The rate of absences would remain the same and the company's production efficiency would not improve.

What the production manager did was to dig up the real reason for the absences. Since the workers were living in close proximity with each other in the province, he tapped their informal leaders. By tapping these men and getting their cooperation in controlling the absences, the manager improved the company's production. The informal leaders would be the social control over the work force to limit their absences to specified periods. The production manager did not change the values of the workers neither those of management; he merely tapped an existing source of social control.

The above example highlights a basic feature of the change process, where the requirements of technologists are often seen as being in direct conflict with prevailing cultural practices and norms. It also shows that Filipino value synthesis is a must if we are to integrate the diverse elements that have seeped into the

148

mainstream of Philippine cultural traditions; and to create an awareness of the basic motivations underlying Philippine behavior patterns—the values, beliefs, and convictions—that bind the people together into a nation with common goals and aspirations. Such an awakening to the cultural ethics and binding principles that Filipinos share is conducive to their sense of national identity and unity, to their growth towards maturity.

Filipino value synthesis is an antithesis to the popular belief that Filipino values are inconsistent with better management policies. Human resources are the most important factor for any organization. They directly affect organizational performance. However, unlike other factors like machines, people's values and attitudes are almost uncontrollable management variables. Hence, management principles involve a thorough consideration of values. After all, management is basically the management of men; and man is a complex of values and attitudes. It is a fact that most business concerns in the Philippines experience problems on the Filipino behavior and its related value system. In most cases, the effects of these problems surmount the difficulties brought about by technical or marketing deficiencies. This is because behavior has a million aspects and combinations such that there can never be a final solution.

Knowledge of the Filipino culture including its values and attitudes is a must for management if it is to do its functions well. It is presumed that the subjects of management are Filipinos, and knowledge of their values and attitudes could help management in the task of managing.

It is noted that motivation stems from the initial statement of management to a subordinate. As such, the approach used in disseminating management's expectation to subordinates shall be most understood and accepted if within the scope of Filipino mentality. Adaptation to employees' feelings and sentiments should never be miscalculated if management wishes to make the employees work to its standards.

Management's concern to reward deserving employees necessitates an objective performance appraisal system. Objectivity refers not only to the system itself but to the person appraising his subordinates. Filipinos, as managers, instinctively tend to be more subjective. The pressures placed by lakad-bata system, utang-na-loob, and hiya have always been present when Filipinos appraise their co-employees. This is one instance where the Filipino values need some redirection. Management may avoid placing employees under officers or senior staff with whom they are related for training, developing, counseling, disciplining, and coaching; so that when the time for performance evaluation comes, there is objectivity. Furthermore, management should not limit promotion to employees with whom they have intangible obligation but rather promote employees based on merit.

Management should have an understanding of the deeply-rooted practices and expectations of their employees whether they appear good or bad. These cultural values can be directed toward the fulfillment of organizational goals provided that they are not narrowly defined in an attempt to imitate the foreign stereotyped efficiency. This cultural awareness in management can help him in his difficult task of deploying people toward the attainment of corporate objectives.

Take the case of the Filipino value bayanihan. Bayanihan is not just any value but it is an embodiment of the best in what is Filipino. It is differentiated from *batarisan* and *balikatan*. Where batarisan means working together for a common purpose but with material gain at the end and balikatan denotes a shouldering of common burden having in mind the mutual advantages, bayanihan means working together for a common purpose, moving forward together, helping neighbors and community, respect for human dignity, and love of God and country.[17] This was the value used by the Filipino forefathers to lay the foundation of the Philippines.

As a type of community life, the bayanihan community is intimate, traditional, sympathetic, and stressing neighborly relationships. The bayanihan community stresses tradition, authority, and the importance of the group rather than the individual. Primary group contacts predominate, which if properly used by management, can be the driving principle behind Filipino sense of belonging to a company. It can give the bone and sinew to companies' productivity program, cost reduction program, work simplification program, and other endeavors wherein the emphasis is on unity, sense of belonging, and service. The bayanihan drives the Filipino to search for a common good and a common goal. It is something money cannot buy because when a Filipino puts *bayanihan* to work, he is imparting a priceless and meaningful part of himself.

A perfect model of Filipino value synthesis for better management is United Laboratories, Inc. which received the "Employer of the Year Award in 1979" from the Personnel Management Association of the Philippines.[18]

United Laboratories, Inc. is a leading pharmaceutical manufacturer in the Philippines. Its products cover wide areas of health and nutrition. Unilab employs 3400 Filipino professionals and skilled workers. It has been in the pharmaceutical business for 34 years and is today number 40 among the top 1000 Philippine corporations.

What made Unilab rise from its humble beginnings to the top of pharmaceutical industry is the story of a management philosophy which, even in 1945 had taken shape and began to permeate all the endeavors of the company. The management developed a system, a way of life of the company, which established that it must rely on the strength of the inherent values, aspirations, and traditions of the Filipino people—the bayanihan way at Unilab.

Bayanihan in Unilab is understood as an embodiment of basic human and Filipino values such as unity, mobility, integrity, truth, equality, and love of God. As the United Creed puts it:

We believe that we are united in thought and action and from this we derive our strength and our spirit of Bayanihan.

We believe in the nobility of our purpose in the service of medicine for the welfare of the people.

We believe that integrity is life for us and to preserve it, we must maintain ethical standards of the highest order.

We believe that truth is our challenge and our search for truth is our contribution to the advancement of medical science.

We believe in equality and justice for all that our greatest asset is our human asset whose endeavors must be given meaning and dignity.

We believe in the Divine Providence whose love has sustained us, whose blessings give fulfillment to our lives.

From the United Lab's Creed, we can see the meaning of bayanihan in the word united. It means genuine concern for every member of the Unilab family as well as the community in which they live. As a system of management, it means many hands and minds working together, each one contributing his share and doing his best for the attainment of a common goal. It speaks not only of enthusiasm, diligence, and team-work. It means working together to their utmost to get a job done, sharing together the fruits of their labor.

151

In practice, bayanihan is looking after the welfare of the lowliest and youngest member, equitable partaking of the fruits of the family's labors, reciprocal material and moral support in time of crisis and emergency, guidance and training of the weaker members, and encouragement and due recognition of the strong members.

Through bayanihan, United Lab's employees are the recipients of the highest benefits in the industry. It was the bayanihan spirit that led management twenty years ago to initiate the Employees' Council, a body composed of men and women representing the different divisions of the company. The council manages the benefits and welfare programs of the employees. In its twenty years of existence, the Employees' Council has successfully evolved a welfare and benefit package that includes the following:

(1) Equitable Profit Sharing System. This enables the employees to share a certain percentage of the company's annual earnings or net profit proportionate to his contribution to the achievement of the corporation's income objective. The amount apportioned among employees is equal to 10% of the profit for the year after all expenses have been deducted.

(2) Quarterly Productivity Incentive Bonus. This is the cash amount given to employees for exerting extra effort. It aims to maximize the productivity of an employee and rewards him correspondingly for his effort thus giving him increase in his earnings.

(3) Christmas bonus, commodity ration, canteen benefit, housing project, hospitalization, maternity benefit, sick leave, vacation leave, marriage benefit.

(4) Discount on drugs, memorial services plan, bereavement aid, retirement plan, insurance plan, savings and loan plan.

(5) Calamity and emergency loan, doctor's services, medicine benefits, educational benefits, athletics and recreational program, and summer program for dependents.

United Lab's management believes that the company's consistent growth has been made possible, more than any other factor, by the collective industry and imagination of the United Lab people themselves who work under the bayanihan spirit. Bayanihan has produced in United Lab a unique spirit of harmony and cooperation, without which it would not become the organization that it is today. Through United Lab's concerted efforts, the company is in constant progress.

This application of the bayanihan value in United Lab proves the principle that an indigenous Filipino value could be tapped to achieve company goals. As we see in United Laboratories, the bayanihan system works in a cycle of give and take, a symbiosis between management and workers, which is, in fact, the whole business of management. This is a challenge to other companies in the Philippines to evolve their own unique management style based on the variety of values held clear by Filipinos. Furthermore, the United Lab experience can indeed be a proof to invalidate the belief that Filipino values run counter to sound management techniques, and should be suppressed if business is to attain progress. This leads to the conclusion that it is not only western social forms and psychological conditions that can give rise to more advanced economic development.

Restructuring Filipino Values for a Genuine Philippine Society

Society is the natural grouping of men who act for a common purpose. That purpose is to live the good life, not only to live but to live well, and in order to live well, man must have a *sufficiency of natural goods*. In societal union with his fellowmen, man not only preserves but perfects his life.

Society is an organic whole and because it is made up of human activity it is a living whole. Although the relation of the member to society is the same as that of the part to the whole, the parts of society are persons whose identity cannot be lost in society. Each part of the social whole has his own value and right. One root cause of many of the Filipino's social problems is the *cultural lag* between Filipino value orientation and social organization. A conflict between two sets of social standards—the ethical and the legal—is evident in numerous citizen-to-citizen and official-to-citizen relationships within social systems of the private and public sectors of Philippine social organization. Ethical rules stress particularistic interests while legal rules emphasize the whole of society's general welfare. Ethical rules which place the family above all other institutions have dominated the value orientation and behavior of the Filipino from precolonial days up to the present. The Filipino has carried overage-laden values and behavior

153

patterns into the present, when such have become socially dysfunctional in today's Philippine social organization.

Fr. Senden gives us as explanation of the Filipino's misdirected behavior his being caught in an insecure social system, a system that is greatly responsible for the negative aspects of his personality and culture, as it does not allow the positive aspects, which he undoubtedly possesses, to erupt. The Filipino seems to be pushed back behind a wall of self-survival and self-defense due to socioeconomic insecurity. Besieged by this atmosphere of extreme insecurity, the positive qualities of the Filipino values are misdirected into negativeness: his religiosity is turned into materialistic pursuit which is turning an ultimate value into an instrumental value; family solidarity becomes exclusivistic and eccentric; self-provision becomes occasion for dishonesty; his perpetual consideration of possibilities leads to ambivalence. This social system in the Philippines based on an unbalanced social structure compels the Filipino to put aside his basically religious, rational, sensitive, refined, efficient, dilligent, and honest inner nature. Self-sufficiency on the part of the Philippine society is the foundation for the development of the Filipino. The restructuring of the value system can create social change. The society is the transmitter of values from one generation to another. Hence, society must have a solid sense and hierarchy of values. Values are goals of society, having as their purpose to render human existence meaningful and to achieve the complete fulfillment of Filipino personality as individuals and as a community.

A society must possess a sound philosophy of values because it must influence the members to the acquisition of right values in life. Man's activity embraces the individual welfare and the common weal. He is an individual person, a valuable member of society. Without society, man is man but not perfectly developed. Man's rationality is a result of a social process. Man's entire mentality is molded by social patterns and man's thinking is done by society. The Filipino as a person is perfected by society. Society must be the means for a good life for all Filipinos.

The Transplant Syndrome: A Philippine Malady

The transplant syndrome is a disease common in underdeveloped countries. This is a disease shared by both the governing and the governed cultures over time. The values and aspirations of those governing, strategized by their unique managerial processes, eventually become the norms of thought and behavior of the governed. Such syndrome is evident in neo-colonialism, stateside mentality, hollywoodization.

Many foreign standards are still being transplanted, subtly and forcibly, into the Philippines—a tragic continuum of the transplant syndrome. This transplant syndrome is pervasive among the educated and urban Filipinos. There is the case of Filipino rich families who send their daughters and sons to the finishing schools in Madrid, Paris, and Geneva who later imbibe the continental style. Another situation is where educated Filipino economists and scientists transplant, sometimes lock-stock and-barrel, the planning formats and managerial systems of highly-advanced western societies.

Can the Filipino not develop a model of his own, rooted in his own environment, compatible with the Philippine context, and in harmony with his values? Filipino values are the mirror of Filipino dreams, the window of his ideas and concepts. Can the Filipino not work out strategies in terms of his own environmental resources, and managing within his own constraints and national goals? Can the Filipino not develop a class of Filipino, Filipino in blood and color, Filipino in taste, in opinion, in morals, and in intellect?

The transplant syndrome has debilitating influence on the Filipino capacity for self-excellence. Motivations based on Filipino values must reshape the Filipino ideological system. Filipino alliances should be formed with the right partners-in-resources based on the Filipino quest for survival, stability, and planned growth. The Filipino must conceptualize, nurture, implement, manage, and evaluate his own development model. Foreign development models and concepts of modernization grew mainly from their own tradition and indigenous environment; these are inherently product of their own internal history and socio-psychological values. These are the natural outgrowths of their own aspirations and goals. Thus, transplanting a foreign development model without experiencing the process of its conceptualization and birth results in a mixture that is often a hodge-podge of unsubstantial imitation. It must be recognized that the Filipino has his own peculiar concerns and aspirations.

Filipino Values Synthesis for the Achievement of National Goals

A country must have a vision of itself. These are its self-defined national values. The will to national consciousness came from traditions, customs, crisis, frustration, and dissatisfaction from values. No people, once inspired by a set of values, want to merely exist in time and space. The reality for all countries today is that each has its own historical setting and its own indigenous social values. From these social values emanate its own chosen national goals.

The developing countries, the Philippines for one, have the following characteristics: dependence on only one or two export products (the Philippines on sugar and copra), the absence of industry, the weakness of the domestic market, the predominance of a ruling class in politics and business, the vast poverty of the masses.

Must the Philippines dream beyond her reach or within her reach no matter how delimited it can be? Must it always have an impossible dream?

National Development and the Spectrum of Values

The Philippines today is undergoing a program of reform. All efforts are being geared toward national development. There is national development if all energies are harnessed towards providing the people "optimum of wealth and a maximum of welfare." This may be attained through the maximum use of time, talent, values, and resources of the Filipinos. The task of accelerated socioeconomic development requires the adaptation of the system to the pulse of society. For this purpose, there is a need for *internal revolution* in the Filipino. Every Filipino has to cultivate values and attitudes on which modernization and development are premised. For instance, Grunner Myrdal in his analysis of poverty in Asia, lists several modern attitudes like efficiency, diligence, orderliness, punctuality, frugality or thrift, integrity and self-reliance, energetic enterprise, alertness to opportunities as they arise in a changing world. He also cites other modern attitudes like cooperativeness, scrupulous honesty, willingness to take the long view, etc.

Cooperation toward national development is a human decision, a decision of an age, of a people. And it takes a people who have shed off their insecurities, inadequacies, and pretenses to pool in their resources for a cooperative endeavor. The Filipinos can meet any problem, so long as they stand together, decide together, and work together.

Basically the Filipino has all the values for the development of the attitudes mentioned by Myrdal for modernization. Of national relevance is the Filipino spirit of cooperativeness which reinforces the channeling of egoistic energy along socially beneficial lines. Like the bamboo, Filipinos have the versatility to be pliant, to bend in crises, only to emerge unscathed after a strong wind. Paradoxically, this is how the spirit of cooperation can work, each Filipino laboring and sacrificing to realize his full potentialities as a human being. A Filipino businessman, for example, should not be interested only in raking in profits but should be conscientious to see that his goods are reasonably priced. On the other hand, the Filipino consumers should not hoard goods or indulge in panic buying to avoid creating undue pressure on supply and thereby prevent price increases. Doctors or lawyers should no longer be prestige-conscious when they serve their patients or clients. Those in authority should no longer be as obsessed in gaining more power but in serving the people.

Politics in the Philippines usually means "my party first and my country second." The Filipino electorate is typically individualistic in its motivation and voting pattern. The question that a candidate must answer, if he is elected, is not "What is in it for me, or my family, or my party?" but "What is in it for the country?" Elections are generally taken as inevitable constitutional directives which have to be fulfilled in any case. There is little thought given to the significance of elections, that is, that they are expressions of the Filipinos' choice of government, direction to be taken towards progress, development, and the fostering of common good. Many have easily surrendered their right of judgment, their exercise of civil freedom by giving their vote in exchange for a price, or by casting it under the sway of emotions or other irrational considerations. It is said that we get the government we deserve. This statement is true, though slightly unfair, for no genuine effort at educating the masses has been made. This effort of education must be free of any political underpinnings if it is to succeed at all. The masses must be made to realize the gravity of their decision to vote; the consequences of the vote upon the progress of the country. Politicians genuinely interested in the welfare of the country must be asked to give their full cooperation to such reeducation projects and part of the off-election energies of parties must be devoted to this work in rural areas, always being careful to remain objective and unbiased: a task admittedly difficult to perform. Citizens with the genuine interests of the nation at heart—free from political ambitions and self-seeking machinations—must bind themselves to the task of opening the eyes of the citizenry to their serious, primary, and God-given role as electors.

The serious duty of exercising the right of suffrage must be instilled in the minds of our people. Besides this, electors have to be made to seek the best men, in the most objective fashion, by stressing the qualities and qualifications candidates for certain offices have to have. These qualities and qualifications must be those permanently required by the office and should not refer to easily-identifiable characteristics of specific candidates.

Men seeking public office must present an objective picture of themselves, their abilities, their preparation for office. Integrity and truth must at all times be preserved. They should be sincere and truthful rather than colorful, deceptive, and cunning. In the end, people respond to truth, sincerity, and goodness. Political groupings must be ready to admit what is good in each other's proposals for the reconstruction of the nation. This means that national reconstruction should be, essentially, a multi-partisan and, in fact, supra-partisan endeavor. President Quezon's classic statement 'My loyalty to my party ends where my loyalty to my country begins' must be the rallying slogan and the fitting description of how government people should behave when confronted with something involving the common good.

There is a lack of a sense of national unity. There is a poverty of idealism among our people. There is a vacuum of sublime causes for our youth. The government, the church and the school, but most especially the family, must provide the Filipino youth with sufficient stimulation, with a world-saving goal to which they could dedicate and identify themselves. Right in their early age, the Filipino youth must be taught to overcome selfishness and acquire the habit of thinking about the welfare of others. The Filipino must be trained to be open-minded and broadminded so as to be ready to accept the gifts of a new culture or insight. In this process of cultural exchange he shall come out richer, without losing, however, his original and valuable heritage of Philippine culture.

One very important thing the Filipinos need is unity. From

the time of the pre-Hispanic period up to the present, the Filipinos are still psychologically and morally disunited. National integration is a must for progress and development. The most effective element for unifying people is a definition of a common purpose, a common goal. In Pilipino, the word *kakampi, kaanib, kapanalig, kaisa,* or *kasama* means ally, associate, colleague, or a partner. This value can be used to promote nationalism. According to Crisol, the inroads of subversion, in meaning and scope, are mainly psychological, based on the destruction of mutual faith between the people and the government established by their own mandate.[19] The four D's of subversion stand for *disappointment, disenchantment, disaffection,* and *disloyalty.* The areas where the subversive war is being waged are in (a) political struggle; (b) economy; (c) social classes; (d) armed conflict; and most important, (e) the hearts and minds of the people. Vulnerabilities and weaknesses, inadequacies and failures are exploited to fan the people's disappointment. The logical result of consistent, persistent disappointment, factual or imaginary, is disenchantment. It is at this point that some people begin to be detached, separated psychologically. Next comes the psychological "point of no return" disaffection, a deteriorated degree higher than the first two. It is at this stage that the people are completely or almost completely "ripe" psychologically to be fanned or whipped into physical action. Disloyalty is the ultimate of the four "D's."

The polishing of Filipino values is primarily a matter of education and it demands a perennial ministry of training the Filipino for a full life of concerned participation in nation-building and development. Develop the Filipino *tao* that he will have faith in himself, in his fellowmen, in his government, in his country. Develop the Filipino tao to bring about mutual confidence with people in the government. This will result in loyalty and unity among Filipinos and the institutions they stand for. This requires national and personal introspection, a critical self-analysis and evaluation.

The central goal of national development should consist of three interrelated objectives: economic growth, self-reliance, and social justice.[20] Economic growth as a form of development to be authentic, must be complete, integral, that is, it has to promote the good of every Filipino and of the whole Filipinos. Development process must create the conditions necessary to provide for the material needs of life at the same time insists on the development of human dignity, values, knowledge, and culture. Development process must create the conditions necessary to provide for the material needs of life at the same time insists on the development of human dignity, values, knowledge, and culture. Development process must not only be economically quantitative but humanly qualitative as well. The development process has been largely patterned after foreign experience; thus lacks the authenticity of being derived from the socioeconomic reality of the country. Attitudes of people, socio-cultural norms, and indigenous management have not been taken into consideration. The qualitative dimension is necessary to ensure a coherent, systematic, integrated approach. Quantum growth must be balanced by qualitative equity to make growth total in dimension and real in human meaning. Thus, concern for values to a degree is as important as economic growth.

The Philippines is rich in a spectrum of values and thus of choices in its pursuit of development which is growth plus qualitative change. For the Philippines, national unity, whereby all sectors of the Filipino people are integrated into one people with a common vision, common values, and positive attitudes, is a must. As a cultural development goal, the Filipino people must define and establish the national identity whereby the vision, strength, cultural uniqueness, and values of the Filipino people would endow this country with a definitive lifestyle and national culture. As an economic and human resources development goal, the Filipino people must create a dynamic, diversified economy and technology of surplus production adapted to Filipino resources and needs. For this purpose, the Filipino values of *pagsasarili, pakikisama, pagkakaisa, pagkabayani*, and *pakikipagkapwa-tao* can be very relevant. A Filipino must have pagsasarili or self-reliance in order to overcome dependency, and, thus be responsible for himself. He must act by himself, think for himself, and possess his own self. It is only then that he can share with others whatever he is; it is only then that he can share with others whatever he owns; it is only then that he can have the value of pakikisama—sharing his human and natural resources with his fellow Filipinos. Sharing or bayanihan will help him and his fellow Filipinos to be self-reliant, independent, and responsible. *Tayo ay makisama upang ang bawa't isa ay makapagsarili.* The natural outcome of the sharing or pakikisama is unity or pagkakaisa. It brings people together into one nation, into one people, into one *bayan* (community). Pagkabayani, which is love of one's country, results to patriotism, total dedication of one's life for one's country and fellow-men. Jose Rizal and Gregorio del Pilar are examples of heroes or *bayani* because they gave their lives for their country. The "Libingan ng mga Bayani" reveals to the Filipino what pagkaba-yani means: it is giving one's blood, sweat, tears, and life for one's country. When Filipinos have learned to give their lives to fellow Filipinos, they have learned the value of pakikipagkapwa-tao or human fellowship. The Filipino should learn not only to become a tao but also how to *magpakatao* and *makipagkapwa-tao*. He should be a brother and a friend to every fellow Filipino.

The Filipino must work hard in order to learn pagsasarili (independence). Pagsasarili is acquired only when there is *kagana-pan* or abundance, *katapatan* or uprightness, *katauhan* or sovereignty, and *katatagan* or purposefulness. The Filipinos must be united into one by having pagkakaisa. They must share whatever they are and whatever they have in the spirit of pakikisama. They must free themselves from ignorance, superstitions, injustices, myths, oppression, and exploitation to be *tunay na malaya* so that they will acquire *kaganapan ng pagkatao*. To do this, they must have *katapatan ng loob* and *katatagan sa layunin* that is, they must be upright and purposeful.

The seven pillars of nationhood are: pride or *karangalan*, loyalty or *kulupatan*, responsibility or *pananagutan*, morality or *kabu-tihang ugali*, self-discipline or *katimpian*, participation or *ugnayan*, and national security or *pagtatanggol sa bayan*.

※

REFERENCE NOTES

[1]Erich H. Jacoby, *Agrarian Unrest in Southeast Asia* (New York: Columbia University Press, 1959), pp. 221-222.

[2]Rodolfo G. Tupas, "Why Filipino Women Are Pampered," *Express-week* (September 6, 1973), p. 11.

[3]Domini Torrevillas-Suarez, "The Filipino Working Women," *Philippine Panorama* (July 7, 1974), pp. 4-5.

[4]Visitacion R. de la Torre, "The Filipino as Lover," *Philippine Panorama* (February 9, 1975), p. 22.

[5]OCR, PA., *Towards the Restructuring of Filipino Values,* p. 41.

[6]Gilda Cordero Fernando, "Coping with the Undomesticated Filipino Husband or No Left Turn," *Woman's Home Companion* (April 19, 1973), p. 6.

[7]Carmen Guerrero-Nakpil, "A Frivolous Talent," Consensus of One, *The Sunday Times Magazine* (October 24, 1971), p. 11.

[8]Ibid., p. 11.

[9]Jaime Bulatao, "Psychotherapeutic Attitudes and Techniques in Nation Building." (Presidential Inaugural Address, Psychological Association of the Philippines, 1965.)

[10]Keynote Speech of Minister Blas Ople at the 16th National Conference of PMAP at the PICC on November 28, 1979.

[11]Jaime Bulatao, *Split-Level Christianity* (Manila: Ateneo University Press, 1967), p. 8.

[12]Jaime Bulatao, "Relevance in Philippine Psychology." (Psychological Association of Philippine Presidential Address, October 11-13, 1969.)

[13]Rosalinda Morales, "Ugaling Pilipino." (An unpublished article for Peace Corps Volunteers, English Section of the Bureau of Public Schools in the Philippines), p. 1-2.

[14]Carmen Guerrero-Nakpil, "The Present Imperfect of the English Language in the Third Largest English Speaking Country," *Expressweek,* (September 8, 1973), p. 14.

[15]Monina A. Mercado, *Fiestas Are Forever,* p. 5.

[16]Morales, "Ugaling Pilipino," pp. 3-4.

[17]Jesus Solomon, "The United Experience," *Industrial Philippines,* Vol. 29, No. 9, p. 16.

[18]Pasig Potentials Group, "Bayanihan in Unilab." (An unpublished research on a Filipino Value as a Management Factor, Ateneo Graduate School of Business, January 24, 1980.)

19Jaime Panesa, "The 4D's of Subversion," *Philippine Panorama* (June 9, 1974), p. 10.

20Ernesto Franco, "Defining National Goals." (Handout distributed at a lecture held in 1978 at Educational Management Center, De la Salle University.)

BIBLIOGRAPHY

A. BOOKS

Agoncillo, Teodoro and Oscar Alfonso. *A Short History of the Filipino People.* Quezon City: University of the Philippines, 1961.

Alvin, Bertrand. *An Introduction to Theory and Method:* Basic Sociology. n.p., 1967.

Andres, Tomas Quintin D. *New Dimensions in Philippine Christianity.* Pasay City: Daughters of St. Paul, 1972.

_____. *Kristiyanismo sa Bagong Lipunan.* Pasay City: Daughters of St. Paul, 1973.

_____ et al. *Sex Education and Family Planning for Filipinos.* Quezon City: Ken Incorporated, 1974.

_____. *Understanding Values.* Quezon City: New Day Publishers, 1980.

Araneta, Francisco. *Values and Institutions for Socio-Economic Reforms.* Manila, Araneta University.

Bassert, Glenn. *Management Styles in Transition.* New York: AMA, 1966.

Batacan, Delfin. *Looking at Ourselves.* Manila: Philippine-American Publishing, 1956.

Bennis, Warren G. *Changing Organizations:* Essays on the Development and Evolution of Human Organizations. New York: McGraw Hill Co., 1966.

Bulatao, Jaime. *The Technique of Group Discussion.* Manila: Ateneo de Manila University Press, 1966.

_____ and Vitaliano Gorospe. *Split-Level Christianity and Christian Renewal of Filipino Values.* Quezon City: Ateneo de Manila University Press, 1966.

Burns, Tom and G.M. Stalker. *The Management of Innovation.* 2nd edition.

London: Tavistock, 1966.

Carrion, J. Antonio. *Salesmanship Imperatives*, Pilot Copy. 1974.

Carroll, John J. *Changing Patterns of Social Structure in the Philippines.* Quezon City, Ateneo de Manila University Press.

Cordero, F.P. and I. Panopio. *General Sociology:* Focus on the Philippines. 1971.

Costa, Horacio dela. *Jose Rizal's la Indolencia de los Filipinos:* An Outline. Quezon City: Ateneo de Manila University Press, 1972.

Davis, Keith. *Human Behavior at Work and Organizational Behavior.* New York: McGraw-Hill Book Co., 1972.

Drucker, Peter F. *The Effective Executive.* London: Harper and Row Publishers, 1967.

_____. *The Practice of Management.* London: Pan Books Limited, 1973.

Duncan, Waler. *Essentials of Management.* New York: McGraw-Hill Co., 1975.

Espiritu, Socorro and Chester I. Hunt. *Social Foundation of Community Development.* Manila: R.M. Garcia Publishing House, 1964.

Ewing, David. *Long-Term Management.* New York: Harper and Row, 1972.

Gaerlan, Josefina E. and Delia A. Limpingco. *General Psychology.* Quezon City: Apson Enterprises, 1978.

Ginzberg, Eli and Ewing W. Reiley. *Effective Change in Large Organizations.* New York: Columbia University Press, 1957.

Gorospe, Vitaliano. *Responsible Parenthood in the Philippines.* Manila: Ateneo de Manila Publications Office, 1970.

_____ and Richard L. Deats. *The Filipino in the Seventies,* An Ecumenical Perspective. Quezon City: New Day Publishers, 1973.

Gowing, Peter G. and Willian Henry Scott. *Acculturation in the Philippines.* Quezon City: New Day Publishers, 1971.

Guthrie, George. *Six Perspectives on the Philippines.* Manila: Bookmark, 1971.

de Guzman, J.V. and Rodolfo R. Varias. *Psychology of Filipinos.* Manila, 1964.

Hicks, Herbert and C. Ray Guilett. *Modern Business Management:* A Systems and Environmental Approach. New York: McGraw-Hill, Inc., 1974.

Hollnsteiner, Mary R.; L. Paglinauan; and Nora S. Villanueva. *Society, Culture and the Filipino.* Trial Edition. Vol. 1, 1975.

Hunt, Chester. *Sociology in the Philippine Setting.* Quezon City: Phoenix Publishing House, 1963.

Irwin Inc., Richard O. *Management of Industrial Enterprise.* 4th edition.

Homewood, Illinois: Richard O. Irwin, Inc., 1963.

Kalaw, Maximo M. *Introduction to Philippine Social Science*. Manila: Philippine Education Co., 1938.

Kassarjian, J.B.M. and Robert A. Stringer, Jr. *The Management of Men*. Manila: Molina's Copier Center, 1970.

Klukhohn, et al. "Values and Value Orientation." In *Toward a General Theory of Action*, edited by Talcott Parsons and Edward Shills. Cambridge, Massachusetts: Harvard University Press, 1959.

Koyama, Kozuki. *Waterbuffalo Theology*. New York: Doubleday and Co.. 1975.

Lardizabal, Amparo S. and Felicitas Tensuan Leogardo (eds.). *Readings on Philippine Culture and Social Life*. Caloocan City: Philippine Graphic Arts, Inc.,

Mallari. *Footnote to Philippine Culture*. Manila: University of the East, 1964.

Marcos, Ferdinand E. *Dialogue with My People*. Manila: Department of Public Information,

Martinez, Esdras. *Supervisory Development: Text and Cases*. Manila: GIC Enterprises, 1973.

Maslow, Abraham. *Motivation and Personality*. New York: Harper and Row, 1970.

Mayo, George Elton. *The Human Problems of an Industrialized Civilization*. New York: Viking Press, 1960.

McGregor, Douglas. *The Human Side of Enterprise*. New York: McGraw-Hill, Inc., 1960.

Mercado, Leonardo N. *Elements of Filipino Philosophy*. Tacloban City: Divine Word University Publications, 1977.

_____. *Applied Filipino Philosophy*. Tacloban City: Divine Word University Publications, 1977.

Molina, Antonio M. *The Philippines Through the Centuries*. Manila, UST Cooperative.

Montemayor, Jeremias U. *Philippine Socio-Economic Problems*. Manila, Rex Book Store.

Myrdal, Gunnar. *Economic Theory and Underdeveloped Countries*.

Nakpil, Carmen Guerrero. *A Question of Identity:* Selected Essays. Manila, Vessel Book.

OCR, PA. *Towards the Restructuring of Filipino Values*.

Ogburn, William S. and Meyer S. Nimkoff. *Sociology*. 2nd edition. Boston: Houghton Misslin Co., 1950.

Osias, Camilo. *The Filipino Way of Life*—The Pluralized Philosophy. Boston: Glenn & Co., 1940.

Randolf, Robert. *Planegement: Movement Concept into Reality*. AMACOM: 1975.

Robbins, Stephen P. *Managing Organizational Conflict:* A Non-Traditional Approach. Englewood Cliffs, New Jersey: Prentice Hall, Inc., 1974.

Roethlisberger, F.J. *Management and Morale*. Cambridge, Massachusetts: Harvard University Press, 1941.

Santos, Rufino J. *The Christian Renovation of Philippine Society*. Pasay City, 1964.

Sayes, L.R. *Human Behavior in Organizations*. Englewood Cliffs, New Jersey: Prentice Hall, Inc., 1966.

Sferra, Adam; Mary Elizabeth Wright; and Louis A. Rice. *Personality and Human Behavior*. New York: McGraw-Hill Book Co., Inc., 1971.

Singson, Jose. *The Art of Fulfilled Living*. Manila: De la Salle University Textbook Committee, 1974.

Tañada, Lorenzo M. *Nationalism: A Summons to Greatness*. Quezon City, Phoenix Publishing House.

Taylor, Edward B. *Primitive Culture*. New York: Brenthenes', 1924.

This, Leslie E. *A Guide to Effective Management*. California: Addison-Wesley Publishing Company, 1974.

Towle, Jose W.; Sterling H. Schdem; and Raymundo L. Hilgert. *Problems and Policies in Personnel Management*. New York: Houghton Mifflin Co., 1965.

Young, Kimball and Raymond W. Mac, *Sociology and Social Life*. New York: American Book Co., 1959.

Zaide, Gregorio F. *Republic of the Philippines*. Caloocan City: Philippine Graphic Arts.

B. MAGAZINES AND OTHERS

Abarzuza, Jesus M. "Philippine Social Values and Suicide." Asian Social Institute, 1966.

Aldaba Lim, Estefania. "Basic Values in Filipino Family Life." *Fookien Times Yearbook* (1962), pp. 241-244.

Alfonso, Felipe B. "The Challenge to Change," *The Philippine Manager* (November-December, 1969).

Alisjahabana, S. Takdir. "Values as Integrating Forces." Unpublished material.

Andres, Tomas Quintin D. "Cultural Values and Its Implications to Education." A study presented to FEU Graduate School in partial fulfillment

167

of the requirement of the course Sociological Analysis of Educational System, 1972.

_____. "Management By Values," *HR Magazine* (May, 1979), pp. 26-30.

_____. "Philippine Cultural Values and Its Implications to Education," *PChC Journal of Educational Research.* Vol. 12, No. 2 (May, 1979), pp. 133-135.

_____. "Management By Values," *Credit Management.* Credit Management Association of the Philippines, 1979.

_____. "Who Is the Filipino?" *Personnel Management Association of the Philippines Newsletter* (January, 1980), pp. 10-11.

Ang, Terry. "Chinese Cultural Values." A Study submitted in partial fulfillment of the requirements of the course in Sociology, De La Salle University, 1975.

Angeles, Cesar et al. "A Study of Philippine Cultural Values and Attitudes in the Context of Business Organization." A Research Paper submitted in partial fulfillment of the requirements of the course Administrative Process and Organizational Behavior, Ateneo Graduate School of Business, December 10, 1979.

Ardales, Venancio B. "A Philosophical Analysis of Philippine Cultural Values." University of San Carlos, 1974.

Azarcon, Cornelio. "Profitability and Productivity," *Carnationews.* Vol. 4, No. 2 (August, 1979), pp. 6-7.

Bayer, Tom. "Management Pegged," *Wichita Journal.* Vol. 94, No. 22, 11.

Beck, Don Edward. "Value Systems Analysis: Implications for Law Enforcement and Criminal Justice." Proceedings, Eleventh Annual Interagency Workshop, Institute of Contemporary Corrections and the Behavioral Sciences, Sam Houston State University, Huntsville, Texas, May 31-June, 1976, pp. 33-40.

_____. "Values for Managing." National Center for Values Research, Inc., Denton, Texas.

Bernad, Miguel. "Philippine Culture and the Filipino Identity," *Philippine Studies.* Vol. 29 (October 4, 1971).

_____. "Western Humanism and the Filipino." Unpublished material.

Bonnevie, Lucille G. "Fashion: Filipino Society." A Position Paper presented in partial fulfillment of the requirement in Sociology course, De La Salle University, January, 1976.

Bulatao, Jaime. "Changing Social Values," *Philippine Studies.* Vol. 10, No. 2 (1962).

_____. "Personal Preferences of Filipino Students." Symposium on the Filipino Personality, Psychological Association of the Philippines, 1963, pp. 7-16.

_____. "Value Orientations of the Filipino Consumer," *Marketing Horizons* (January, 1964).

_____. "Hiya," *Philippine Studies.* Vol. 12, No. 3 (1964).

_____. "Psychotherapeutic Attitude and Techniques in Nation Building." Presidential Inaugural Address, Psychological Association of the Philippines, 1965.

_____. "The Hiya System on Filipino Culture," *The Philippine Educational Forum.* Vol. 14 (1965).

_____. "Filipino Subjective Values," *Philippine Progress.* Ateneo University, 1968.

_____. "The Manileño's Mainsprings." In *Four Readings on Philippine Values,* edited by Frank Lynch and Alfonso de Guzman II. Ateneo de Manila Press, 1976.

_____. "Relevance in Philippine Psychology." PAP Presidential Address, October 11-13, 1979.

Bulatao, Rodolfo A. "Some Philippine Beliefs and Practices Related to Fertility," *The Value of a Filipino Child*—Pleasure and Profit against Cost and Concern. Manila, 1976.

Carroll, John J. "Filipino Entrepreneurship in Manufacturing." In *Four Readings on Philippine Values,* edited by Frank Lynch and Alfonso de Guzman II. Ateneo de Manila University Press, 1968. pp. 87-113.

_____. "The Filipino Heritage." Unpublished material.

Castro, Norma. "The Cultural Values Affecting the Guidance Program in Cavite City Public Elementary Schools." National Teacher's College, 1972.

Catarroja, Sebastian. "Virtues and Vices of the Filipino Family," *Philippine Panorama.* Vol. 1, No. 19 (December 8, 1974).

_____. "The Permanence of Change," *Philippine Panorama* (December 15, 1974), 9.

Cordero-Fernando, Gilda. "Coping with the Undomesticated Filipino Husband or No Left Turn," *Woman's Home Companion* (April 19, 1973), 6.

Costa, Horacio de la. "Reflections on Philippine Economic Development," *The Journal.* American Chamber of Commerce, 1976.

David, Randolf S. "Human Relations on the Waterfront: The Cabo System," *Philippine Sociological Review.* Vol. 15, Nos. 3 and 4.

Dia, Manuel A. "Socio-Psychological Factors Affecting Productivity of Skilled Workers." A Paper read during the National Manpower Congress for the Eighties, Philippine International Convention Center, January 24, 1980.

Elevazo, Erwin A. "The Supervisor and the Filipino Worker." A Study submitted in partial fulfillment of the requirements in Administrative Process and Organizational Behavior, Ateneo Graduate School of Business, August 28, 1978.

Fernando, Deogracias A. "The Tyranny of AWA in Personnel Management," *PMAP Newsletter* (March-April 1975), 3.

Flores, Jimmy. "A Study in Suicide: The Filipino as a Fatalist," *The Sunday Times Magazine* (June 23, 1968), pp. 44-48.

Fox, Robert B. "The Filipino Concept of Self-Esteem," *Area Handbook on the Philippines*. Chicago Human Relations Area Files, 1956.

_____. "Ancient Filipino Communities," *Filipino Cultural Heritage*. Philippine Women's University, 1966.

Franco, Ernesto A. "Management, Pinoy Style," *HR Magazine* (May, 1979), pp. 21-24.

_____. "Defining National Goals." Unpublished material.

_____. "A Dilemma Over Values," *HR Magazine* (May, 1978), 11.

Gorospe, Vitaliano R. "Christian Renewal of Filipino Values." Ateneo de Manila University, 1960.

Graves, Clare W. "Human Nature Prepares for a Momentous Leap," *The Futurist* (April, 1974), pp. 72-85.

Group II of APOB Class 1979. "Filipino Values and the Practice of Management in the Philippines." A Study presented as partial fulfillment of the course Administrative Process and Organizational Behavior, Ateneo Graduate School of Business, April 5, 1979.

Hall, Rich. "Individual's Value Sets Affect Job Performance," *Wichita Journal*. Vol. 94, No. 22, pp. 1-10.

Hollnsteiner, Mary R. "Social Control and the Filipino Personality," *PSR*. Vol. 2, Nos. 3 and 4 (1963).

_____. "Reciprocity in the Lowland Philippines." In *Four Readings on Philippine Values*, edited by Frank Lynch and Alfonso de Guzman II. Ateneo de Manila Press, 1976, pp. 22-49.

Innovators Syndicate, The. "Filipino Values and Attitudes." A Research Paper submitted in partial fulfillment of the course Administrative Process and Organizational Behavior, Ateneo Graduate School of Business, 1979.

Jocano, F. Landa. "Filipino Social Structure and Value System or in Filipino Cultural Heritage." In *Management of Men*, edited by J.B.M. Kassarjian and Robert A. Stringer, Jr. Manila, 1971.

_____ and Luz Policarpio Mendez. "Social Values," *The Filipino Family in Rural and Urban Orientation*. Centro Escolar University Research and Development Center. pp. 213-215.

_____. "Social Control and Value Orientation." *The Filipino Family in Rural and Urban Orientation*. Centro Escolar University Research and Development Center. pp. 178-184.

170

Karingal, Ramon V. "The Filipino: His Values and Attitudes." A Study submitted in partial fulfillment of the requirements of the course Administrative Processes and Organizational Behavior, Ateneo Graduate School of Business, August 28, 1978.

Ledesma, Feliciano J. "Educators Must Help Give Our Children True Cultural Values."

Lentigas, Angeline M. "Family, Community and Religious Values of Residents of Dulo Puting Bato." Asia Social Institute, 1974.

Ligouri, M. "Moral-Spiritual and Socio-Cultural Values in a Filipino College Students Group, Implications for Individual Study." *The Guidance and Personnel Journal* (1966), pp. 37-38.

Lopez, Julian. "The Filipino as a Planner." A Research Paper on Management, University of the Philippines, 1968.

Lynch, Frank (ed). "Social Acceptance," *Four Readings on Philippine Values.* Ateneo de Manila University Press, 1968. pp. 1-21.

_____. "Understanding the Philippines and America," *A Study of Cultural Themes.* IPC, 1968.

_____. "Social Acceptance Reconsidered." *Four Readings on Philippine Values.* Ateneo de Manila Press, 1976.

Madhab, Pradyuet. "Indian Business Venture in the Philippines." A Study submitted in partial fulfillment of the course Administrative Process and Organizational Behavior, Ateneo Graduate School of Business, 1979.

MBA-SEP (Guevent) et al. "Behavioural Problems in Introducing Change in Philippine Business Organization." A Research Paper submitted in partial fulfillment of the requirement of the course Administrative Process and Organizational Behavior, Ateneo Graduate School of Business, 1979.

Mercado, Monina A. "Fiestas Are Forever."

Morales, Rosalinda. "Filipino Traits," *The Philippines and You.* Philippine Commercial and Industrial Bank, 1972.

_____. "Ugaling Pilipino." Unpublished material.

Munsayac, Bella R. "The Influence of Four Selected Filipino Values on the Acceptance of Family Planning among Selected Army and Navy Couples." The Philippine School of Social Work, PWU, 1978.

Nakpil, Carmen Guerrero. "Will Success Spoil the Filipino?" *The Sunday Times Magazine* (September 21, 1969), 19.

_____. "Filipino Cultural Roots and Foreign Influences." Lecture delivered during the 15th International Conference on Social Welfare on its seminar on Socio-Economic Perspectives on the Philippines, Davao City, September 2-5, 1970.

_____. "A Frivolous Talent," *The Sunday Times Magazine* (October 24, 1971), 11.

_____. "Filipinos Are Wild Drinkers," *The Sunday Times Magazine* (October 31, 1971), 15.

_____. "The Present Imperfect of the English Language in the Third Largest English Speaking Country," *Expressweek* (September 6, 1973).

Ocho-Carim, Paz. "Attitudes of Selected Muslim and Christian College Students Towards Certain Family Values." Notre Dame University, 1976.

Pal, Agaton P. "Ideal Patterns and Value Judgments in the Development of Program Planning," *Silliman Journal.* 2nd Quarter (1960). .

Panesa, Jaime. "The 4D's of Subversion," *Philippine Panorama* (June 9, 1974).

PAP. "The Philippine Value-System and the Filipino Personality." Unpublished material.

Pasig Potentials. "Bayanihan in Unilab." A Research on a Filipino Value as a Management Factor submitted in partial fulfillment of the requirement of the course Administrative Processes and Organization Behavior, Ateneo Graduate School of Business, January 24, 1980.

Quirino, Liesel C. "Filipina for Women's Movements," *Woman's Home Companion* (December 4, 1975), 9.

Quisumbing, Lourdes R. "Philippine Cultural Values and Development." Unpublished material.

Ramirez, Angelina. "Humanizing the Work Environment." A Speech delivered on the occasion of the University of Santo Tomas Foundation Week, Manila, January 21, 1978.

Ramirez, Mina. "The Filipino Family, Philippine Institutions and the Value System." Unpublished material.

Roces, Alfredo R. "Light and Shadow," *The Manila Times* (October 27, 1965).

Romulo, Carlos P. "The Search for Filipino Identity: Its Nature." Unpublished material.

_____. "The Filipina Manager," *HR Magazine* (September, 1979), pp. 7-10.

Ruiz, Macario B. "Value Orientations of Central Philippine Faculty." *Southeast Asia Journal.* Vol. 7, No. 2 (1974), pp. 1-25.

Santiago, Cynthia U. "The Filipino Manager," *HR Magazine* (May, 1979), pp. 15-19.

Santos, Carmencita C. "A Literature Research on Supervisory Behavior." A Term Paper submitted as fulfillment of the requirement in Human Behavior in Organization, University of the East, Graduate School of Business Administration, 1977.

Santos, Vicente Sumajit, Jr. "KAKAMPI, In Search of Identity," *Philippine Panorama* (October 9, 1977), 26.

Senden, Francis. "Positive Aspects of Philippine Values." Unpublished material.

Solomon, Jesus. "The United Experience," *Industrial Philippines.* Vol. 29, No. 9 (November, 1979).

Soria, Estanislao A. "Toward Identifying the Values and Positivising the Negatives." Unpublished material.

_____. "Toward Identifying Filipino Values: A Preliminary Report of the Institute of Mass Communication." Unpublished material.

Stewart, Helen. "Value Systems Analysis," *The Management Journal of Atlantic Richfield Company.* Vol. 2, No. 5, pp. 15-20.

Sytangco, Ramon A. "The Chinese Among Us," *Philippine Panorama* (February 9, 1975), 4.

Tanjutco, Edgardo. "Restructuring the Philippine Value System." Unpublished material.

Tombo-Velarde, E. "Relationship of Values and Intelligence of College Students in Central Luzon." UST Graduate School, 1967.

de la Torre, Visitacion R. "The Filipino as Lover," *Philippine Panorama* (February 9, 1975), 22.

Travina, Mirriam M. "A Study of Relationship Between Wives' Developmental Value Orientation and Their Fertility." Central Philippine University, 1977.

Valencia, Teodoro F. "The Compadre System," *Expressweek* (September 6, 1973), 6.

_____. "The Image of the Filipino Through Foreign Eyes," *Expressweek* (June 27, 1974), 6.

Varias, Rodolfo R. "Psychiatry and the Filipino Personality." Symposium on the Filipino Personality, Psychological Association of the Philippines, 1963.

Ventura, Sylvia Mendez. "Why the Filipino Should Walk Proud," *Woman's Home Companion* (August 2, 1973), pp. 15-17.

Villaraiz, Alex A. "The Philippine Social Values in Relation to Management and Organization." A Study submitted in partial fulfillment of the requirements of the course Administrative Processes and Organizational Behavior, Ateneo Graduate School of Business, August 21, 1978.

Villegas, Bernardo M. and Carlos A. Abola. "Towards a More Productive Filipino Worker (Or Why Is There No Filipino Word for 'Productivity'?)." A Progress Report on a Research Project partially funded by Asia Foundation, May, 1974.

_____. "The Management of Human Resource in Organization." A Paper read in celebration of the National Budget Week at the Philippine International Convention Center, April 25, 1978.

_____. and Antonio N. Torralba. "Studies on Motivation and Productivity (Or Understanding Filipino Workers Through Eyes of Foreign Social Scientists), Part I." Center for Research and Communication, August, 1974.

_____. "Studies on Motivation and Productivity (Or Understanding Filipino Workers Through Eyes of Foreign Social Scientists), Part II." Center for Research and Communication, September, 1974.

Villote, Ben J. "The Filipino as Contemplative," *Philippine Panorama* (March 16, 1975), 13.

Vivar, Teofista L. "The Moral-Spiritual Value Preferences of Teachers of Public Secondary Schools in Manila." University of the Philippines, 1971.